Slim

Slim
Michael Calvert

Pan/Ballantine

Editor-in-Chief: Barrie Pitt
Editor: David Mason
Art Director: Sarah Kingham
Picture Editor: Robert Hunt
Designer: David Allen
Cover: Denis Piper
Special Drawings: John Batchelor
Photographic Research: Jonathan Moore
Cartographer: Richard Natkiel

Photographs for this book were especially selected from the following Archives: from left to right pages 2-3 Imperial War Museum, London: 9-11 Royal Military Academy, Sandhurst: 12-19 IWM: 22 Keystone Press Agency, London: 23-29 IWM: 30-31 United Press International, London: 32 IWM: 32 Fujifotos, Tokyo: 33 IWM: 36 Sado-Opera Mundi, Belgium: 37 US National Archives, Washington: 38-45 Fujifotos: 46-47 IWM: 47 Pictorial Press, London: 50-53 IWM: 54 Brigadier Calvert Collection: 56 IWM: 57 Popperphotos, London: 58 IWM: 59 Calvert: 59-60 IWM: 62-63 National Archives: 62-63 Keystone: 63 IWM: 64-65 Shigeo Fujii Collection, Japan: 66-67 IWM: 68-69 Sado: 72-73 IWM: 74 Mujifotos: 74-77 IWM: 78 Popperphoto: 78-81 IWM: 82 Fujifotos: 82-84 IWM: 86 Popperphotos: 87 IWM: 89 Popperphotos: 89 Fujii: 89 Fujifotos: 94 Fujifotos: 95 IWM: 96 Keystone: 102-103 IWM: 102-103 US Army, Washington: 104-105 IWM: 106 Fujifotos: 107-111 IWM: 112-113 Calvert: 113 Keystone: 114-116 Calvert: 117 US Army: 121-122 IWM: 123 Keystone: 124-131 IWM: 132 US Army: 133-158 IWM: 158 Radio Times-Hulton Picture Library, London.
Front cover: US National Archives, Washington: Back cover: Imperial War Museum, London

Copyright © Mike Calvert 1973
ISBN 0 345 09788 2

First published in the United States 1973.
This Pan/Ballantine edition first published
in Great Britain 1973.

Pan Books Ltd, 33 Tothill Street, London, SW1.
Ballantine Books Ltd – an Intertext Publisher.

Printed by Cox & Wyman Ltd London & Fakenham

Contents

8 Independent spirit

12 Gallabat and Deir-ez-Zor

24 The retreat from Burma 1942

46 XV Corps and the Arakan

54 A new look at the war

60 Raising morale

68 Japanese offensive

84 Imphal-Kohima

110 The Blackpool plan

120 The reconquest of Burma

British bulldog
Introduction by Lieutenant-Colonel A J Barker

In the depressing days of April 1942 a young British officer, Major Michael Calvert, introduced that master of unorthodox soldiering, Orde Wingate, to the bluff commander of the newly-raised XVth Indian Corps, Lieutenant-General Slim. Wingate said after the meeting: 'There is only one soldier worthy of the name East of Suez. He is a bad-tempered little terrier by the name of Slim.' What seems to have impressed Wingate, aside from Slim's self-evident confidence and coolness, was his complete failure to be either impressed or irritated, as many senior officers were, by Wingate's purple past and deliberate outlandishness.

Wingate's appellation 'terrier' might be considered appropriate – though most of us who knew Bill Slim would consider bulldog a more fitting label; bad-tempered he was certainly not. Indeed it was his gruff, genuine, no-bloody-nonsense sort of humour, which had such an appeal to soldiers. Even when things were really bad his sense of humour never deserted him. Finding his officers at Burcorps HQ rather despondent during the retreat from Burma in 1942, he said 'Cheer up. Things might be worse!' 'How could they be worse?' somebody asked. 'It might be raining,' said Slim. At that moment it came on to rain.

Slim's sense of humour was only one of the personal qualities which brought him the devotion of his subordinates. Compounded with it was a complete and simple naturalness, and a down-to-earth approach to men and events. He was ready to speak personally to every man under his command from general to private soldier, and when he did speak – in English, Gurkhali, Urdu or Pushtu – it was always as one man to another, never as the great commander to his troops. As a Second-Lieutenant in the 9th Battalion The Royal Warwickshire Regiment he had taken to heart the military principle that an officer's first duty is to care for the welfare of his men. In those early days, however, his application of the rule was often too literal and unorthodox for the peace of mind of his superiors; and at that time nearly everyone was a superior. There was, for instance, the occasion in Mesopotamia when he ran some risk of court-martial for sheep stealing. Best of all, as an illustration, is an adventure that happened in Gallipoli in the summer of 1915.

The Warwicks were resting, which meant that instead of manning the trenches under fire its members were gathered beneath the cliffs on the seashore, still under fire from the Turkish artillery and in conditions of discomfort little better than those they had been forced to endure in the trenches. By some stroke of luck – the sort of 'luck' that he had a habit of making happen – Lieutenant Slim had managed to secure for his platoon the one patch of shade on the whole stretch of beach where a large rock stood detached from the main cliff. Here his men flung themselves down to snatch an hour of well earned sleep, while a platoon from another regiment was forced to swelter nearby under the blazing Gallipoli sun. There is no reason to suppose that Slim was any less weary than his men and most officers in his position would have 'got down to it' themselves.

Why did not Slim? Perhaps some sixth sense that most great leaders possess and learn to heed sounded a warning. As it was, instead of relaxing he stood out in the sun watching the spasmodic shelling of the beaches by a far-off invisible Turkish gun. Noticing that each exploding shell was nearer than the last, he concluded that the fourth shell from then would fall in the very shadow of the rock under which his men were lying. Most people, having so decided, would have taken the line of least resistance and said in effect 'it may not happen'. But there was no such word as 'may' in Slim's vocabulary. Once he was sure of his calculations he did not hesitate to take the hard and unpopular way. He awakened his platoon sergeant and explained the situation, and the two of them set about getting the men out once more into the brassy glare of the sun.

There was almost a mutiny. Worn out and heavy with sleep, the men resented being driven from the only shady spot they had seen for days. But by dint of persuasion and hard swearing it was achieved at last. The men squatted glumly in the open, swearing profusely and cursing all meddlesome officers with bees in their bonnets, while, amid much rejoicing and deaf to all warning, a platoon from another regiment dropped down in their place and were asleep in a moment. In due course the fourth shell arrived, and a number of that unlucky platoon never woke again.

Nearly thirty years later the same concern for his troops' welfare enabled Slim to restore the self-respect and confidence of an army in whose defeat and anguish he had shared. How he led the same army back to victory constitutes the main theme of this biography. Considering the personalities with whom he had to deal, the fact that he was so successful may be attributed to his refusal to shut his eyes to unwelcome truths, reinforced by an uncommon dexterity in the difficult borderland between diplomacy and strategy. Whether anyone other than Slim could have managed Wingate, maintained the respect of that toughest of nuts, General 'Vinegar Joe' Stilwell, or remained so unswervingly loyal to his dashing and elegant superior Lord Louis Mountbatten, is questionable. Inevitably there were disagreements, but Slim was far too loyal and soldierly a man to reveal them publicly.

Success never went to his head, and he remained modest and approachable to the end of his days. Some years ago when I was writing a critical analysis of the operations round Imphal I asked his opponent, General Mutaguchi, how he explained the Japanese defeat. Mutagushi's answer in effect, was that Slim had out-generalled him. When I told Slim, his dry response was that 'Japanese generals – possibly not unlike other generals – always make out the best case for their success or failure.'

In 1948 Slim was appointed Chief of the Imperial General Staff. At that time there was probably no other soldier possessing the character and experience to handle the difficult problems confronting the professional head of the British army. When his appointment terminated two years later, he said to me: 'It's not a bad job; I commend it to you.' As a junior officer I had already come to doubt the theory about the field-marshal's baton hidden in my knapsack. But at that moment my confidence surged. To me, and to countless others, no other general had the same appeal as Bill Slim. Thousands of those who had the privilege of serving under him – British, Indian, and his own beloved Gurkhas – will remember him as the finest general the Second World War produced.

Independent spirit

William Joseph Slim was born in Bristol on 6th August 1891 and was educated at King Edward's School, Birmingham. From early boyhood, he showed great interest in the army but his father could not afford to send him to Sandhurst nor support him financially when he joined a regiment, as was necessary in the British army at that time, so Slim became an employee of the steel firm of Stewart and Lloyds in Birmingham.

Because of his keenness, he was allowed to join the Birmingham University Officers' Training Corps although not a member of the University. Joining of necessity as a private, Slim was soon promoted to lance corporal. There is no truth, therefore, in the wartime public relations exercise that he rose from the ranks of the regular army.

Three weeks after the start of the First World War on 4th August 1914, Slim was commissioned as a Second Lieutenant. After initial training he was posted to the 9th Service Battalion of the Royal Warwickshire Regiment which became part of the British 13th Division.

In June 1915 this division was sent to the Dardanelles and took part in the abortive assault on the Turkish defences at Sari Bair on 9th August. In this assault the company in which Slim was serving as a lieutenant came in contact with some Gurkhas of the 1st/6th Gurkha Rifles. His own battalion suffered severely in the attack and Slim himself was wounded in the shoulder.

Slim was invalided back to England and, after convalescence, was posted to the holding battalion of the Royal Warwicks from which drafts were sent to reinforce battalions overseas.

Meanwhile the 13th Division had evacuated Gallipoli and taken part in the Mesopotamian campaign along the Rivers Tigris and Euphrates. Slim was drafted back to his old regiment, leaving England in February 1916. He was given the command of a company. During a long and dreary campaign in the desert Slim became favourably impressed by the courage, staying power and humour of the British soldier, especially when faced with uncongenial terrain and on the lowest priority for arms and equipment. This understanding of the British soldier was to stand him in good stead later on. Most Indian army officers lacked this advantage, and found it correspondingly difficult to handle British troops in action, being used only to Indian sepoys drawn from an unsophisticated village background.

During this campaign in Mesopotamia Slim was wounded again, this time in the arm, and was awarded the Military Cross for 'valour in the face of the enemy'. However he continued to serve with the Royal Warwickshire Regiment for the remainder of the war.

After the end of the war Slim transferred to the 1st Battalion 6th Gurkha Rifles. In the Gurkha depot he first had to learn to speak Gurkhali and familiarise himself with the background and characteristics of the redoubtable mountain-dwelling Mongolian soldiers. He was appointed adjutant of the 1st Battalion in 1922.

In the battalion at that time were G A P Scoones, D T Cowan, D D Gracey and J B Scott, all young captains or subalterns. Scoones was to become a Lieutenant General commanding IV Corps at Kohima in 1942-44 and later became a full general in India in 1945-46. Cowan took over the 17th Indian Division on the retreat from Burma

Above: Lieutenant-Colonel Slim (front row, second from right) in a Staff College group in 1935 *Below:* Slim (second from right) in the Gare du Nord in 1934

in 1942 and remained its commander until the end of the war. Gracey commanded the 20th Division, also part of IV Corps at Imphal. Scott commanded Slim's other division on the Burma retreat, the 1st Burma Division and later became Inspector of Infantry in India in 1943. These officers, all of the 1st 6th Gurkhas, were to maintain a close cabal throughout the Burma campaign which was to make Slim famous. They remembered their smart firm adjutant who was a bit of a martinet as he helped his colonel reorganise and reform his battalion for peacetime duties. This entailed converting a superb wartime fighting machine into a smart polished display unit capable of withstanding the rigours of peace with all its temptations and softness. However, frequent essays into the fighting on the North West Frontier of India kept the battalion's martial feet on the ground so that its officers did not become too theoretical in their outlook on war.

In 1925 Slim became a student of the Staff College Quetta. Staff College students were expected to be good riders to hounds. Slim was not. This fact may have saved him from becoming too hidebound and too much a servant of the establishment, as he was thus forced to maintain an independence of character and individual spirit. He concentrated on learning the art of war methodically and this was to stand him in good stead all his life.

After further regimental and staff soldiering he had the good fortune to be selected as the one Indian Army representative on the teaching staff at the Camberley Staff College in England. He obtained this post through consistently good work and good appearance (which was always considered necessary in peacetime). But he still maintained an independence of thought which raised him above his fellows. General Sir Archibald Nye, a fellow instructor, says that he gave the impression of stability, solidity and reliability. These may not sound like the characteristics to fit a man for high command, except of the Blucher type. But Nye, who was a good judge of character, goes on to say that he had two qualities to a very high degree – complete integrity, and a good intellect.

This latter quality must be judged by comparison with his fellow officers. The British army did not normally attract men of high intelligence. Its more intelligent officers were usually men who had entered the regular army through the back door, as Slim had done, or university entrants and sons of wealthy families who entered the Guards or Cavalry. With private incomes behind them, these men could afford to hold independent and unorthodox views which the impecunious infantry officer could not.

Slim's main attribute was a down-to-earth practical approach to problems, sweeping aside verbiage and the undergrowth of 'ifs' and 'buts' to get to the root of the matter.

After his three years as instructor at the Camberley Staff College, Slim was chosen in 1937 for the one-year course at the Imperial Staff College. Here he had the chance to meet and work with navy and air force officers and senior civil servants besides those of his own kind from the British army – an experience of inestimable value to his later career, as it liberated his mind from the unavoidably narrow confines of the Indian army. The Imperial Staff College was founded to study the science of warfare – its civil, economic and diplomatic as well as purely military aspects. In practice it fell short of these mature geopolitical targets, but it certainly strived towards them.

Slim was forty-six by the time he had completed this course. It was considered essential in the British and Indian armies that an officer, in order to reach high rank, should command a battalion at some time in his career so that, while considering

Lieutenant-Colonel A E Nye (left) during a mountain warfare exercise

the upper strata of command, he should never forget that all plans and orders have to be carried out in the end by simple men with all their faults and virtues.

Slim was very fortunate, therefore, after five years in England to obtain command of the 2nd Battalion of the 7th Gurkha Rifles. After only eighteen months in command he was made Commandant of the Senior Officers' School in India.

On the outbreak of the Second World War in September 1939, he was appointed to command the 10th Indian Infantry Brigade formed at Jhansi in Central India. This brigade at first had no motorised transport and few trained drivers. It had no wireless sets, no armoured fighting vehicles, no anti-aircraft or anti-tank guns and only a few obsolete automatic weapons. In fact it was totally unfit for modern war. Indian army military thought, with a few notable exceptions, was still based on Boer War tactics of forty years before.

Slim, with his British army training, used every device and improvisation to overcome his brigade's deficiencies. He trained a good staff under him and inspired his battalions even if he could not at once give them modern material and teach them technical skills. After a year of training, by which time its deficiencies in weapons and equipment had been partly made up, Slim's 10th Indian Infantry Brigade sailed as part of the 5th Indian Division to the Middle East. There they were to face their first enemy, the Italian and Colonial regiments who formed the Italian army of occupation in Eritrea, Somaliland and the recently Italian conquered Ethiopia. Slim was now forty-nine.

Gallabat and Deir-ez-Zor

Below: Australian tanks advance into Syria, June 1941. *Above*: British troops parade in the Sudan in 1940. *Below right*: Blenheims over North Africa

In June 1940, on the heels of the German *Blitzkreig* which overran Holland, Belgium and France, Italy declared war on Great Britain, and General Wavell's Middle East Command was faced by apparently overwhelming Italian forces in Libya and East Africa. The Commander-in-Chief of Italian East Africa had 250,000 troops at his disposal, including sixty tanks and 250 aircraft. But of these, seventy per cent were colonial troops and the morale of his white troops, seemingly cut off from their homeland in a war which they did not want, was low.

1,500 miles away from Wavell's Headquarters in Cairo, the British forces in the Sudan comprised 4,500 all ranks without any artillery but including three British battalions. There were also three squadrons of obsolete Wellesley bombers, a squadron of Blenheims and six obsolescent Gladiator fighters.

General Platt, in command in the Sudan, offensively manoeuvred this small force to make the Italians believe that it was 20,000 strong; and since Wavell believed in subversion and guerrilla warfare as a means of weakening the enemy, military missions were infiltrated throughout Ethiopia to support the local resistance movements.

Platt was delighted when he heard that the 5th Indian Division had been diverted from its original destination, Iraq, and was landing at Port Sudan in the Red Sea in September 1940. This division consisted of only two brigades, each comprising three Indian battalions, but the artillery was British manned. Platt placed his three British battalions under divisional command to form a third brigade, and spread the experienced British battalions so that there was one attached to each brigade.

Brigadier Slim's 10th Indian Infantry Brigade was sent to Gedaref, about 100 miles north of the border town of Gallabat which was to be their first objective. They were supported by 28th (British) Field Regiment artillery and one squadron of the Royal Tank Corps consisting of six cruiser and six light tanks. They also now had nineteen Gladiators in support, accompanied by all the available Wellesley bombers.

The Italians had captured and occupied Gallabat in July 1940. Their defences there consisted of Gallabat Fort and the defended village of Metemma, both strengthened with field defences, barbed wire and anti-tank mines. These two defended areas sat on knolls each side of a dried river bed which formed the frontier between Sudan and Ethiopia, and they were in a position to support each other by fire. The Italian garrison comprised four Colonial battalions strengthened by two companies of Blackshirt machine gunners. There was also a hetereogenous collection of mortars, artillery and light anti-tank rifles.

The strength of the opposing forces was about the same, but the British had the advantage of British-manned artillery and tanks and a higher proportion of European infantry. In the air the Italians were superior, since their Fiat CR42 fighters were more modern than the Gladiators.

By early November the British had 28,000 troops in the Sudan, and a general advance from the Sudan and Kenya was ordered by the British Cabinet. Slim was ordered to capture Gallabat. Though in itself a comparatively minor operation, it was at that moment the only British offensive taking place anywhere in the world.

The attack began at dawn on 6th November. After a heavy bomber attack, the resistance at Gallabat Fort was quickly overcome by the British and Garhwali battalions attacking alongside the tanks and by 0730 hours the success signal went up. The artillery fire lifted to shell the defences of Metemma. But four out of the six cruiser tanks and five of the light tanks had been disabled by anti-tank mines. Slim had failed to put in his sappers and miners in advance to clear a way for the tanks.

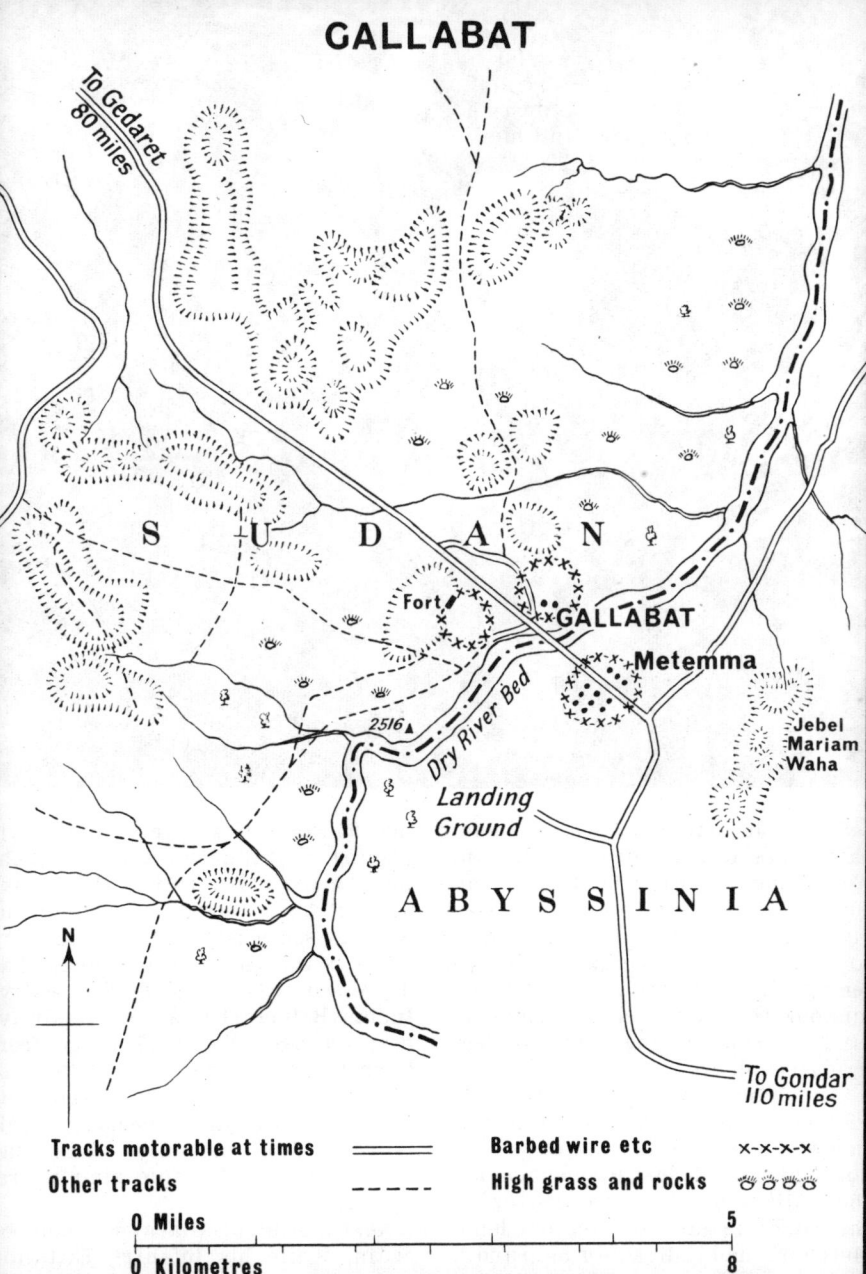

Slim had left his reserve Indian battalion too far to the rear. The tank commander reported that after capturing Gallabat some of his crews had dismounted to examine the damage to their tanks. Some Indian troops, seeing them in their black berets mistook them for enemy soldiers and fired on them, killing many of these irreplaceable troops.

Slim himself went up to Gallabat to reconnoitre. This reconnaissance turned out to be a false move as by so doing his attack lost momentum and the Italians had time to recover. By this time the garrison commander at Metemma had radioed for help and in the afternoon about thirty Italian bombers and fighters bombed and strafed the newly taken Gallabat Fort. The Gladiators took off to intercept but five out of six were shot down, leaving the Italians in command of the air. Among other things the Italian aircraft destroyed the lorry coming up with the spare parts for the tanks.

The evacuation of the wounded had depressed the morale of the reserve Indian (Baluchi) battalion. It is always best to keep wounded away from fresh troops as they usually tend to give an exaggeratedly depressing account of a battle, especially if this is their first encounter. Slim had neglected to take this simple precaution.

Next morning Gallabat was bombed again. While his infantry battalion commanders and his artillery commander tried to persuade Slim to continue the attack, Slim was swayed by a Quetta Staff College trained brigade major who favoured caution, and ordered a withdrawal. Slim had lost forty-one men out of his 4,000 strong force and 125 wounded. Most of the casualties were incurred by the British battalion which, with the tanks, had borne the brunt of the fighting.

Why did Slim order the retreat so soon after so few casualties? To understand this we must examine the Indian Army methods of fighting in the North West Frontier of India. There it was considered a crime for a battalion or brigade commander to risk casualties and, if he incurred more than a very small number, he could be removed from his command. One reason for this was that the Indian Army, due to continual political unrest, was thought to be a more brittle structure than in reality it was. Also almost too personal a relationship had been built up between officers and men so that a commanding officer not only knew the names and background of the men under his command, but knew their fathers and families too. Casualties were the yardstick of success or failure and on the North West Frontier there was always time to fight again next year if necessary.

This factor was deeply imbued in the Indian Army Officers' make-up and accounted for early retreats, lack of determination in attack and unaccountable surrenders in the first few years of the war.

Slim, in spite of his British army training, had absorbed much of this peacetime attitude and it took some years before he shook it off. In his despatch on the Gallabat operation he presented his defeat as a victory, but he admitted the truth to himself and learned from his mistakes, so this initial failure was to make him a better general. From this time on he would always try to choose the bolder course in battle.

The Italians stood firm at Gallabat until 1st January 1941 when they withdrew, pursued by a mobile detachment of 9th Indian Infantry Brigade who had taken over from Slim's 10th Brigade. On 3rd January General Wavell ordered General Platt to go on and take Keren and Asmara.

General Platt, reinforced by the

Below: The Sudan Defence Force at bayonet practice. *Left:* Artillery in action in Abyssinia, November 1940

Above: Some Italian colonial troops captured during an abortive attack on Gallabat in November 1940. *Below:* Destroyed Italian tank

Above: General Wavell with Australian Lieutenant-General Laverack and Major-General Allen in Syria, June 1941. *Below:* Allied forces enter Damascus, June 1941

battle-hardened 4th Indian Infantry Division from the Western Desert, began his advance from the Sudan into Eritrea on 19th January. The 4th Indian Division led the advance. The task of 5th Indian Division was to secure a base at Aicota, a small township on the road to Keren and Massawa. From there Major General Heath sent Slim's 10th Infantry Brigade to cut the enemy's retreat at Keru, held by the Italian 41st Colonial Brigade. On 22nd January the Italian native brigade withdrew but not before Slim, who boldly advanced, cut up its headquarters. The Italian commander, his staff and 800 others were captured.

The battle for Keren which followed in February and March 1941 sealed the fate of the Italians in Eritrea.

Keren fell on 27th March. Slim was not there to see it having returned to India after being wounded in the buttocks whilst sheltering from an Italian air attack. He did not return to his brigade but after a short time as a GHQ India staff officer he was promoted to Major General to command 10th Indian Division.

At this time Syria was coming increasingly under the influence of the Germans who were using it as a base to stir up trouble amongst the Arabs in Palestine and all over the Middle East. The British Government decided to eliminate this influence in Syria by invasion. In Syria there were 45,000 Vichy French forces including 20,000 colonial troops, with about ninety tanks.

Wavell at that time was fighting in the Western Desert, Abyssinia and in Greece and Crete, so his forces were fully stretched.

After some argument Wavell organised a force consisting of 7th Australian Division (two brigades only), 5th Indian Infantry Brigade, six battalions of Free French, a British commando, and some horsed and mechanised cavalry regiments. They were to find the going hard as the Vichy French fought valiantly from cleverly sited positions. By 18th June 1941 Damascus had fallen to the Allies but the main French position was based on the Litani River on the coast. Two Indian battalions of the seasoned 5th Indian Infantry Brigade had fought very well and had between them incurred 738 casualties.

But on 21st June the Vichy French were faced with a new land front. 10th Indian Division, under the command of Major General Slim had taken over northern Iraq and were in a position to threaten Vichy French communications between Damascus and Homs. The French position throughout Syria was now in peril, and Palmyra fell on 6th July.

Slim, having now received sufficient transport, was ordered to advance his unseasoned division to capture the bridge and trade centre at Deir-ez-Zor, reputedly held by 400 French colonials with artillery in support. Slim was supported by 127th Fighter Squadron. He advanced in two columns, one following the line of the Euphrates and the second sweeping around from the south, with his third brigade in reserve. The distance from his base at Haditha to his objective was about 150 miles.

Dust storms and some bombing delayed the advance of his raw brigades. Slim was not going to risk defeat so he deployed two whole brigades in a deliberate operation to capture this rather weakly held village.

He sent one detachment consisting of the 13th Lancers, a troop of artillery and the 4 13th Frontier Force Rifles to circle round and cut off communications from Aleppo to the northwest. When this had been done his plan was to attack in two brigade columns from the east and south.

By 1st July his Euphrates column from the east came under long-range artillery fire and halted. On the left flank, the encircling columns bogged down owing to dust storms, lack of petrol and poor navigation. So Brigadier Weld, commanding the southern column (21st Brigade) ordered them

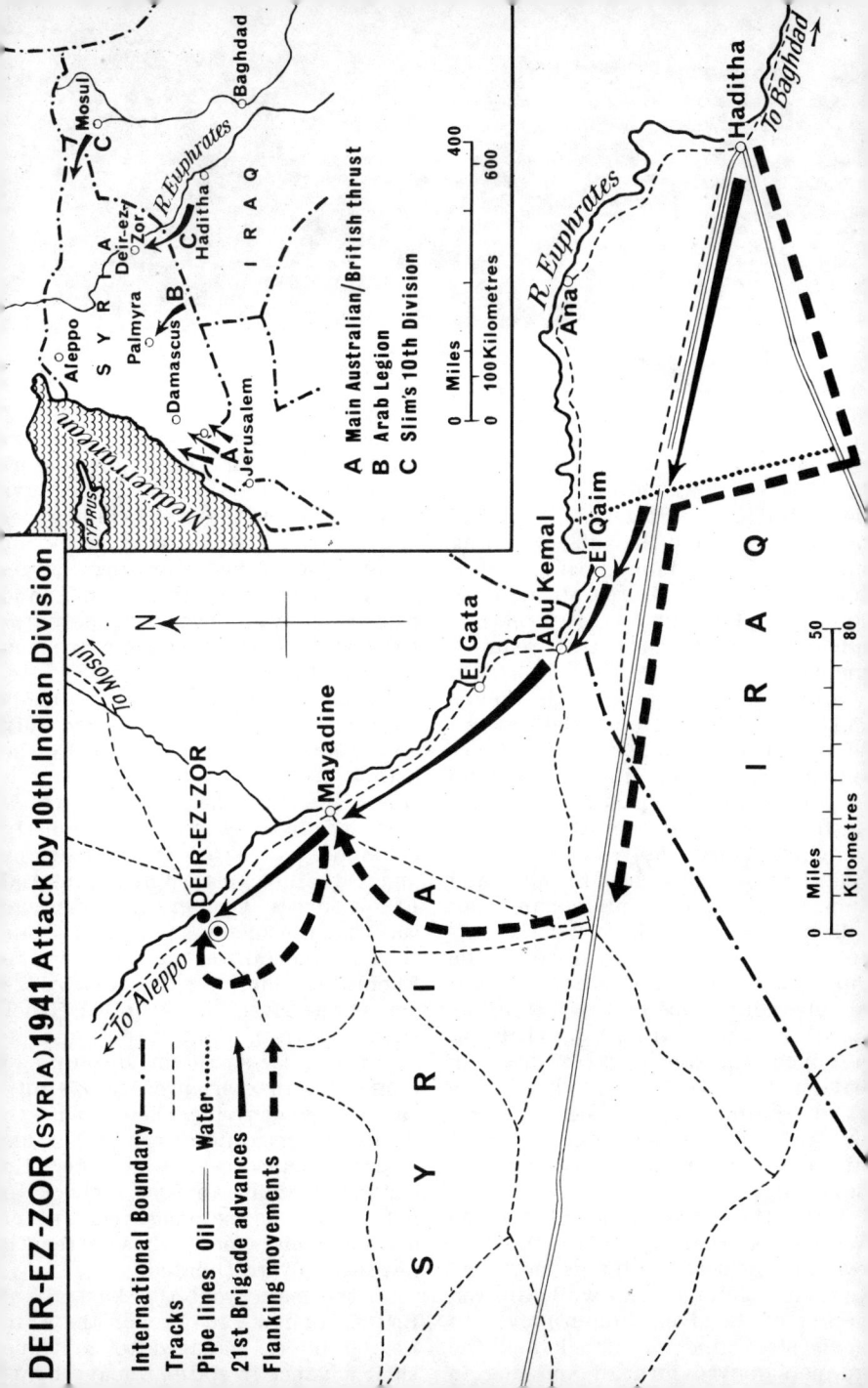

to concentrate with his main force. Slim had kept out of the way so as not to breathe down his subordinate's neck. But on hearing that Weld had become stuck and that his encircling movement had failed, Slim leaped into a jeep and motored all night to join him. He found that Weld had underestimated his petrol requirements.

Slim did not agree with Weld's modified plan of attack, and ordered his senior administrative officer, Lieutenant-Colonel Snelling, to send up all the petrol he had. Snelling managed to scrape together 5,000 gallons, which arrived the same evening. Snelling was a master of resource and improvisation and – unlike many staff officers – stuck to the belief that his job was to serve the fighting men. His rule was that administrative staff should work twice or three times as hard as fighting troops, as they did not incur the same risks of death in battle. He was later to be Slim's chief administrative officer throughout the Burma campaign, and gave him continual efficient and energetic support.

When the petrol came, Slim made Weld stick to his original plan. That evening the desert columns moved off to their appointed tasks while Gurkha troops of the river column moved to their start line for attack and the gunners moved forward and dug in their guns.

The enemy garrison had been weakened when their 2nd Light Desert Company made a sortie some days before, meeting the Arab Legion under Glubb Pasha. The Legion at once made an unorthodox bloodcurdling charge, killing eleven of the enemy and capturing five officers and seventy-two men for only one of their own men killed and one wounded.

The attack on Deir-ez-Zor was made at dawn on the morning of 3rd July and was soon over. Surprised by the attack from the north-west simultaneously with the expected attack from the east, the enemy, mostly colonials, evacuated their positions and fled. Slim captured nine guns and 100 prisoners. One great advantage was that the enemy had not had time to blow the railway bridge over the Euphrates which was the only bridge across the river for 100 miles either way.

In this quite small action Slim had nursed his inexperienced troops into battle, manoeuvring them so as to apply the maximum number of his forces in support of each other. He could not afford another setback in his career; so he made certain of defeating his enemy whose strength he greatly overestimated.

On the main front the Australian, British, Indian, Free French and Arab Legion forces managed to continue their advance in spite of heavy fighting on the river lines of the Litani and

Australian battery under fire from Vichy French artillery, Merjayoun, Syria

Damour. By the evening of 11th July the French General Dentz ended hostilities and a convention was signed at Acre, and the Free French General Catroux assumed control of the civil administration. The Syrian campaign had lasted five bitter weeks.

The British forces lost 3,300 including prisoners whom they regained. The Free French lost about 1,300. The Vichy losses were about 6,000 of whom about 1,000 were killed. The RAF lost twenty-seven aircraft.

Slim saw no further fighting from July 1941 to March 1942 when he took over command of Burma Corps after Rangoon had fallen to the Japanese.

During the intervening period he kept the peace in Iraq and his division was moved into Persia where they met the Russians. It was essential that Persia, with all its oil, should not fall into German hands. The Russians were falling back into the Caucasus and there was little to stop the advance of the Germans except space, logistics and active guerrillas to their rear. So Russia and Britain divided up Persia between them and uneventfully occupied it. Persia became a route along which Britain could send arms and supplies to the Russians. Two 'class 70' concrete roads (taking up to seventy ton loads) were built from south to north to carry these supplies to Russia. They continued to be used for the next three years. Slim saw this road building and was impressed by what modern heavy road construction equipment could do. The roads were mostly built by Americans, and later, in Assam, Slim was to use their example in urging his British engineers to push forward the roads which he vitally needed to support his troops at the front.

Burnt-out Vichy French armoured cars

The retreat from Burma 1942

The Japanese attacked Pearl Harbor, Singapore and Hong Kong on 7th December 1941. Landings in the Philippines and Malaya followed. On 8th December the Japanese Fifteenth Army entered Bangkok. They crossed into the lower extremity of Burma at Victoria Point a few days later, and on 20th January 1942 the Japanese invasion of Burma began.

Thus the war moved into the region where Slim was to fight for the next three years. Burma is isolated geographically by a great horseshoe of jungle-covered and malaria-infested mountains, ranging up to 7,000 feet (and 20,000 in the north), which surround it on the west, north and east. Uncrossed by any vehicular road until the Burma road to China was built, these mountains are inhabited by peoples of good fighting potential – Kachins, Chins, Shans and Karens – who were very loyal to the British. In the middle of the horseshoe, the plains of the Irrawaddy and its tributary the Chindwin stretch 900 miles south to the sea at Rangoon. The southern part of this plain, the Irrawaddy delta, is cut into paddy fields with a few jungle-covered hills; the centre, around Mandalay, is a dry zone of arid sandy country, suitable for tanks; further north, the country becomes more rugged, and merges into the numerous mountain ranges, with a rainfall of 80-200 inches a year.

For the Japanese, an invasion of Burma had certain attractions. Firstly, they were very much concerned with China, and hoped that by knocking out its last link with the West, the 2,000 mile long Burma road, they could force Chiang Kai-Shek to come to terms; conversely, one of the main aims of the Allies, especially of the USA, was to keep China fighting and thus tie down twenty-six Japanese divisions which might otherwise be used elsewhere. Secondly, occupation of Burma by Japan would protect Japanese conquests to the east and south;

Japanese infantry advance into Burma

it should be easy to hold, surrounded as it was by nearly impassable mountain ranges, but with good internal communications which would allow a mobile defence on interior lines to defeat any thrust in turn. Thirdly, though less important, Burma had some oil fields, and produced a vast surplus of rice when the crops could be harvested during settled conditions.

The Japanese Fifteenth Army which carried out the invasion consisted of the 33rd Division of three infantry regiments (equivalent to British brigades) and the 55th Division of two infantry and one cavalry regiment, comprising altogether 35,440 men, equipped with 701 horses, 53 troop-carrying vehicles, and 570 trucks, but no tanks.

In addition, the Japanese 5th Air Division held air dominance over the skies of Burma throughout the retreat; the RAF during this period was largely engaged in assisting the navy in the Indian Ocean.

At the outbreak of war with Japan, the Burma Army consisted of two British and four Indian battalions, about eight Burma Rifle battalions, and three Indian mountain batteries of artillery, with supporting troops. In December 1941 it was reinforced by 16th Indian Brigade, and in early January by 17th Indian Division which took over 16th Brigade.

The condition of these troops was appalling. The Burma battalions were recently formed and ill-equipped; with one or two exceptions they turned out to be unready for modern war, and could not be relied on to hold positions. The Indian army had not mobilised to any great extent since 1939 because of the internal political situation. 17th Division's regular battalions had been milked to the last drop for reinforcements to the Middle East, Malaya and infantry training centres, and were sent into Burma composed largely of recruits who in some cases had joined the battalion only hours before embarcation. In 16th Brigade, for example,

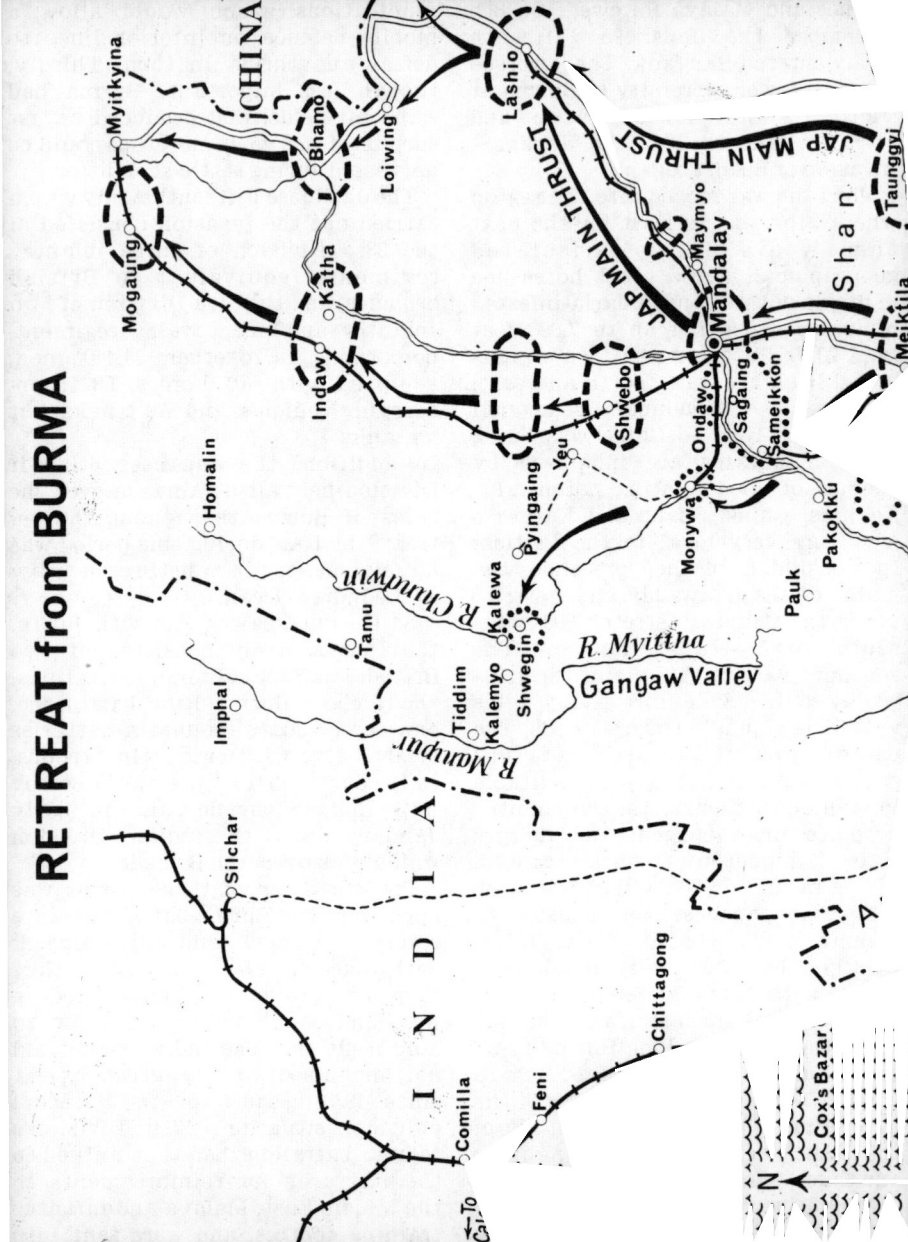

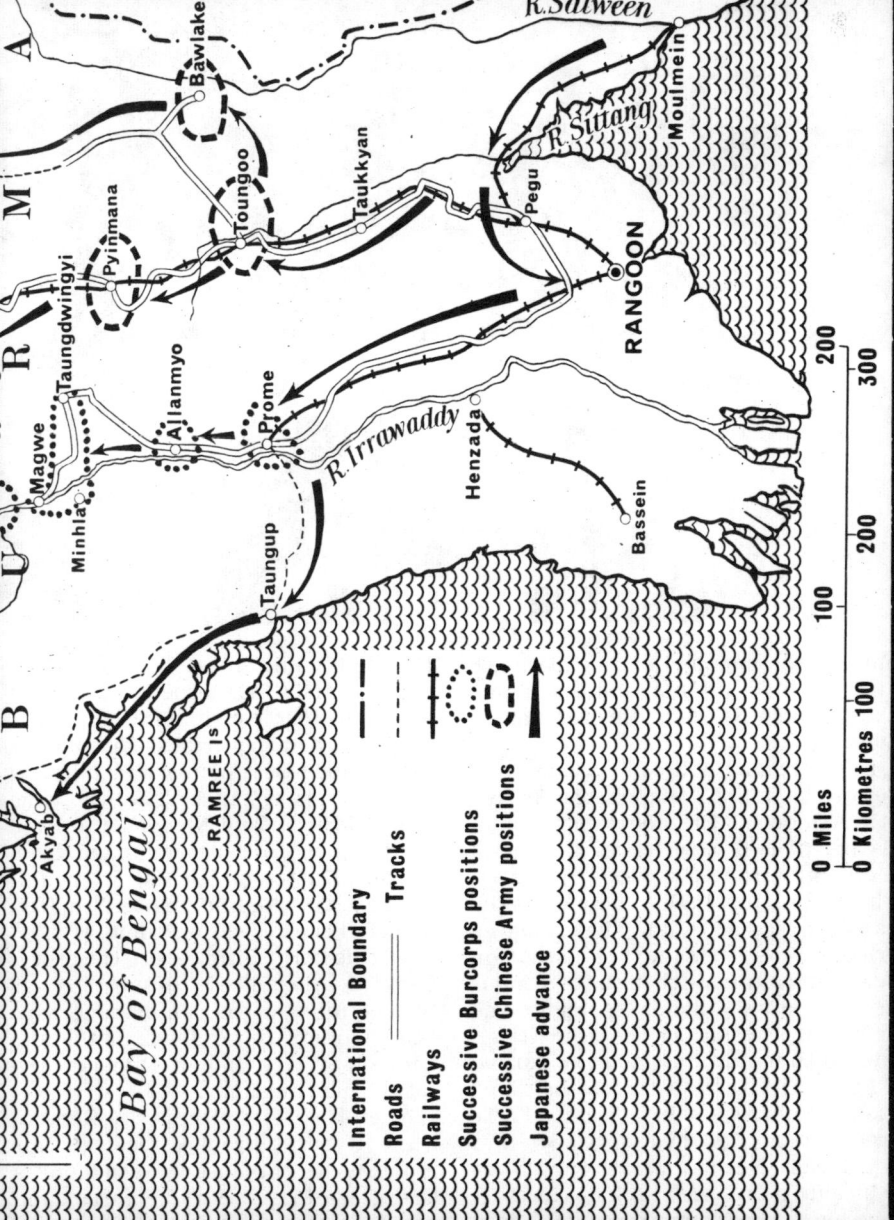

most of the men had little experience of firing live ammunition and none, except some NCOs. of throwing grenades.

In the second half of February, just before the fall of Rangoon, the British 7th Armoured Brigade landed, consisting of two experienced armoured regiments from the western desert. This was an invaluable addition as the Japanese had no tanks. The armoured brigade was to save the situation again and again, although its armour became more difficult to apply and bring into action as the retreat fell back into mountainous north Burma.

In all the British forces including staff numbered about 120,000. These troops were pushed forward into south-east Burma, where they were soon cut off or forced back by the swift enveloping movements of the Japanese. After the disaster on the Sittang river on 23rd February, when a key bridge was blown leaving two brigades on the far bank, the 17th Division could muster only eighty officers and 3,404 other ranks (out of about 16,000 men) of whom only 1,420 still had their rifles. Throughout this period losses in men and material were very heavy indeed. By the time General Sir Harold Alexander arrived in Rangoon to take command from General Hutton on 5th March, the fall of the city was imminent. 17th Division fell back towards Prome.

At this point Slim enters the story. General Alexander's first step was to ask for a corps commander with headquarters to be flown in to take control of 17th Indian Division and 1st Burma Division.

When the Chief of Imperial General Staff, General Brooke, received this request, he intended to send out a first class British service corps commander who had studied European war. But Slim's old friend and one-time colleague and fellow instructor, General Nye, remembered this outstanding Gurkha officer and put

Above left: Indian troops in training.
Above: General Wavell, Supreme Commander, South West Pacific
Left: Major-General Nye, Vice-Chief of the Imperial General Staff

forward his name, stating that having had experience with both British and Indian troops, he could understand them and improve their morale which was the most important factor in jungle fighting in a remote area, with a low priority in supplies. He thought that Slim, who had not shown any particular brilliance as yet, was just the man to carry out a long retreat: he was stubborn, he had an indomitable spirit and, like the British troops, he never knew when he was beaten. He looked the part, too, with his prominent jaw and tight lipped mouth, and he had the trust and confidence of the Gurkhas who were to play an ever increasing role in the battles ahead.

It was thus that on 19th March 1942, Slim took command of Burma Corps ('Burcorps') based on Prome, on the western route leading from Rangoon to Mandalay. 17th Division was already retiring on Prome. 1st Burma Division had been deployed all along Burma's eastern frontier with Siam, in case the Japanese came that way. Now that the Japanese had played their hand, this area could be left to the reconnaisance troops of the Burma Frontier Force. Alexander's plan was to hold the Japanese on the line of Prome-Toungoo, astride the two roads north from Rangoon. There was an eighty-mile jungle-covered hilly gap between these two towns, with no connecting roads. Two Chinese armies were moving south to Toungoo to block the eastern route.

These Chinese 'armies', which now entered Burma, approximated to British divisions in strength; their divisions were equivalent to British brigades and their regiments to battalions. They were good troops with years of experience in fighting the Japanese. But they had two failings. Firstly the command structure was complicated so that General Alexander had to transmit his orders via the American General, 'Vinegar Joe' Stilwell and then on to the

The Japanese occupy Rangoon Docks

Major-General D T Cowan, commander of 17th Indian Division after the fall of Rangoon

Lieutenant-General Shojiro Iida, commander of the Fifteenth Army and conqueror of Burma

Chinese army commanders, who could appeal to Generalissimo Chiang Kai-Shek in faraway Chungking if they did not like these orders.

Secondly, Chiang Kai-Shek's policy was to keep these divisions, which were part of his central army, as opposed to the Chinese provincial armies, intact and to keep his armies 'in being'. Chiang Kai-Shek always had his eye on the time when after the war he would need these armies to fight the Communist leader, Mao Tse Tung, to decide who should rule China, – Chiang's Nationalists, or Mao's Communists. The result was that the Chinese fought by manouevre in ways and means which were alien to the orthodox courageous straightforward minds of Generals Alexander and Slim. So they soon lost their faith in the reliability of these Chinese armies.

On the other hand the Chinese had offered to come to the help of Burma a month or two before. Wavell agreed. They blamed the British for this delay and the piecemeal use of the Chinese forces in the battle for Burma. Their opinion of the fighting prowess of British and Indian commanders and troops was also understandably low after the debacles in Singapore and Hong Kong.

Slim found that conditions at his Burma Corps Headquarters were difficult. His signal detachment was scraped together from Burma Headquarters and had only four wireless sets whose batteries had to be recharged by operating a pedal driven generator. Transport was scarce, and trained staff officers were few. This was, however, a blessing in disguise, as it meant that his headquarters was small and therefore very mobile. The one great disadvantage Slim faced was lack of reliable communications with his two divisions, although excellent communications were obtained with 7th Armoured Brigade which was Slim's real trump

Spitfire in Burma

card, if he could use it.

Slim's two divisional commanders, Major General D T Cowan who had just taken command of 17th Division and Major General Bruce Scott of 1st Burma Division had been fellow junior officers together with him in the 6th Gurkha Rifles. So they were 'in each others minds' which is the best form of communications of all. Short messages only had to be sent and Slim could rely on his subordinates to interpret them as he wanted.

The gap between Prome and Toungoo was impassable to Burcorps who had only recently been taught to fight from a multitude of vehicles, which they collected around them in the British manner, whereas it was an ideal arena for the Japanese who were taught to march and fight on their feet and whose forte was rapid infiltrating and encircling movements.

Slim took over command in truly depressing conditions. 1st Burma Division had not yet been relieved at Toungoo by the Chinese. 17th Division, though re-equipped from the abandoned arsenals in Rangoon, was still shaken by its Sittang experience. Slim felt, however, that if he could concentrate his two divisions he could help restore morale by a counter-attack and advance. The enemy had no answer to his tanks.

The Japanese commanders' orders were to bring the British and Chinese armies to battle before Mandalay and destroy them. Special attention was to be paid to the destruction of the Chinese armies whom the Japanese feared most, especially after the poor showing by British and Indian troops in Malaya.

Within a week of receiving his instructions General Iida, the Japanese commander of Fifteenth Army, had made his plan. Two fresh divisions (18th and 56th) and two tank regiments were on their way, but he decided not to wait for them. He decided to advance up the two routes with 33rd Division on the left against Slim at Prome, and 55th Division on the right to capture and encircle the Chinese concentrating at Toungoo, by a wide flanking movement through the Shan States. The Japanese had about 400 aircraft to support this attack. The remains of the RAF were concentrated at Magwe, between Prome and Mandalay, but without the early warning system which had been left on the airfield at Rangoon. The RAF attacked a Japanese concentration of aircraft on the Mingaladon airfield near Rangoon, but the next day the Japanese in turn caught them on the ground at Magwe and practically wiped them out. The few remaining aircraft flew out to Akyab on the Bay of Bengal. The Japanese now had total command of the air over Burma, and concentrated on destroying railway communications, road and rail bridges and river steamers on the Irrawaddy. They also bombed Mandalay and the summer capital, Maymyo, where Alexander's headquarters were situated.

These attacks caused panic in these towns and most of the Indian, Burmese and Chinese inhabitants departed; only the Anglo-Indians and Anglo-Burmese stuck to their posts and continued to man the railways, river steamers, and post and telegraph offices.

On 29th March Slim was ordered to launch an attack (without any determined objectives) to relieve the pressure on the Chinese at Toungoo. 17th Division was not yet fully reorganised and 1st Burma Division was still concentrating at Allanmyo forty miles to the north. Slim attacked with the depleted 17th Division supported by 7th Armoured Brigade.

The attack failed disastrously in spite of the good work carried out by the armour, and the infantry recoiled in confusion and near rout. One elderly humorist from the First World War put up a notice on the road north of Prome saying 'All last survivors of battalions report here'.

The Japanese then followed up on

either flank and put road blocks on the only road leading north from 17th Division's position. Only determined attacks from the armour broke through these road blocks and allowed 17th Division to withdraw once more to the north.

On one occasion the Japanese strapped a young good-looking British cavalry officer to a road block and dared the British tank to fire. The British fired, destroyed the block and their own officer. On another occasion the Japanese west of the Irrawaddy encountered a part of a British force which had successfully raided Henzada behind their lines. The Japanese overwhelmed this force capturing seventeen men whom they stripped and lined up for bayonet practice. A sergeant major and a private named Williams (a Welshman) made a break for it and, although wounded, swam the Irrawaddy and brought the news of these Japanese to Slim's headquarters nineteen miles away.

Slim was forced to withdraw. His corps now entered the dry belt in the hottest time of the year with temperatures up to 110°F and water difficult to find. Although this was more suitable terrain for tanks, neither division nor their commanders, nor, in fact, Slim himself had had any experience of fighting with an armoured brigade and they tended to use the tanks in penny packets with widely dispersed detachments of infantry, more to support their morale than for any deep thought out tactical reasons.

Wavell, who had come to Burma to meet Alexander and Stilwell on 1st April told the British Prime Minister that the complete Japanese command of the air was setting the Allied commanders in Burma an extremely difficult task. On 5th April Alexander cabled Wavell that the lack of any air support was already adversely affecting the morale of the troops. The following day, in a personal letter, Alexander admitted that the state of morale of his troops was causing him anxiety. The 17th Division, he said, was tired and dispirited, and consequently did not fight well at Prome. Lack of air support meant that Alexander and Slim had no means of carrying out air reconnaissance over enemy held territory in Burma and had to rely entirely on ground patrols for information.

As the Official History states of this period: 'The stage was set for the main battle for Central Burma' with everything in the enemy's favour. The Japanese army was homogeneous, with undisputed air superiority and, with sea communications secure and with control of the port of Rangoon, could easily be reinforced. The Allied armies, on the other hand, although ostensibly under a single commander, served two masters, for the Chinese only obeyed orders countersigned by their Generalissimo. The Allies were almost entirely without air support, and the British Forces were bound to diminish in strength and efficiency as the campaign continued since they could be neither reinforced nor re-equipped.'

17th Burma Division withdrew through 1st Burma Division who were now deployed thirty miles south of the Yenangyaung oil fields near Magwe. 17th Division, less one brigade which was used to give close protection to the oil fields, was put on 1st Burma Division's left flank. The armour was now concentrated in the centre with one regiment with 17th division. This was effected by 8th April.

The Japanese 33rd Division soon penetrated this long linear front between the two divisions and established a block on the Pin Chaung north of Yenangyaung. The Japanese had again avoided roads and marched to this objective thirty or more miles behind the British position. 1st Burma Division, now rather demoralised and carrying their wounded, tried, with the aid of tanks, to break the block. They only escaped due to a counter-attack by the Chinese 38th Division. But the Burma Division left behind it half its strength and most of its guns

Lieutenant-General Stilwell marches north through Hukawng Valley

and transport of which the Japanese soon made use. This acquisition of transport, however tended to make the Japanese stick to roads and to slow them down.

The Chinese took some persuasion to put in an attack but when they did they showed excellent use of ground and minor tactical skills which was an object lesson to the British and Indian troops who saw them.

Slim presented an indomitable and unshaken front in the face of these disasters, and his rather ponderous jokes cheered his staff and commanders when they were at their lowest ebb.

Slim now gathered his force together and, with the aid of the Chinese 38th Division, was determined to attack the now strung-out Japanese 33rd Division in the rear.

But on 19th April, General Alexander called a conference with Slim and Stilwell to explain new orders from General Wavell in India. Wavell said that if total withdrawal from Burma was inevitable, 1st Burma Division

Japanese troops with their folding bicycles advance on Lashio

must stick by the Chinese as, for political reasons, it was essential to prevent Chiang Kai-shek from saying that he had been deserted by the British. So the Burma Division must be redirected east towards the Burma Road and Lashio.

Slim asked if he might undertake his attack with both the Chinese 28th Infantry and Chinese 200th Mechanised Division. He was told he could go ahead.

But in the meantime the Japanese 55th Division had secretly thrust right through the Shan States to the east of the Burma plain and threatened Lashio on the Burma Road. The Chinese promptly and naturally retreated to cover this position which was their lifeline to China.

This they did without orders from General Stilwell. On one occasion to make the 200th Mechanised Division attack and recapture the village of Taunggyi Stilwell had offered the Commander 50,000 rupees (about £7,000) if they took it that evening. The bribe proved effective and the

Japanese infantry pass abandoned British carriers in Burma

village was recaptured before dark.

Some Chinese divisions could not reach China in time and had to retreat all the way to the north of Burma and out over a monsoon-flooded track along the Hukawng valley to Ledo in north-eastern Assam. The tough sixty-year old General Stilwell took this arduous route on foot.

So Slim was left without his experienced Chinese forces.

Burcorps was now ordered to retreat via Kalewa to India. Slim had forwarded these orders to his divisional commanders on 26th April.

There were three routes of withdrawal. The first was along the malarial Myittha Valley to Kalemyo. Slim had heard that the Japanese might use this track to seize Kalemyo. This would be disastrous to the British as it would cut their retreat to India, so Slim sent 2nd Burma Brigade up this route. Alexander ordered Slim to send one other brigade by river steamer up the Chindwin to hold Kalemyo. This left 1st Burma Division with only one brigade, so one of the three brigades of 17th Division was placed under its command.

The second route to India was astride the Chindwin to Monywa. 1st Burma Division would take this route.

The third way out was across the Sagaing railway bridge over the Irrawaddy and north to Shwebo Ye-u and then west to Shwegin and Kalewa to Kalemyo. The two brigades of 17th Division with the 7th Armoured Division would take this route. As long as the monsoon held off, the sandy tracks along this road were just able to take loaded vehicles. This was the main route of the retreat of some 250,000 Indians from Burma to India, and caches of food were laid

Oil storage tanks blasted by Japanese bombers in Burma

along the road to assist them. Cholera and other diseases broke out amongst the refugees and this via dolorosa was littered with corpses and those left to die.

By taking this route the 17th Division could still keep contact as far as Mandalay with the remainder of the Chinese divisions.

When these orders were issued, Burcorps was stretched between Pakokku on the Irrawaddy near its junction with the Chindwin, and Maiktila, fifty miles east on the Rangoon-Mandalay railway. Corps Headquarters was at Sagaing, ten miles west of Mandalay.

The Gurkhas of 17th Division fought a rearguard action at Kyaukse before crossing the Irrawaddy at Sagaing.

By 30th April both divisions had crossed the Irrawaddy and a span of the huge bridge at Sagaing had been blown, and as many boats as possible destroyed or sent up river.

On the evening of the 30th April 1st

Burma Division started its move to Monywa.

The pursuing Japanese 33rd Division did not advance up the Myittha Valley but, after occupying Pakokku and Myingyan, the advance guard of one regiment reached the west bank of the Chindwin opposite Monywa on 1st May. Other battalions moving up the river in landing craft also arrived at dawn on 1st May but fortunately did not cross over to Monywa.

Some 2,400 clerks and Indian servants who were proceeding up river by riverboat were fired on when passing Monywa and this was the first indication Slim received of the Japanese whereabouts. If, as Slim now feared, Monywa had fallen, the Japanese would then be able to cut all routes to India; it would also mean that the Japanese were between his Corps Headquarters and his divisions. So he ordered 1st Burma Division, with one squadron of 7th Armoured Brigade to concentrate and attack. He also ordered 48th and 63rd Brigades to move by rail to join them. The 17th Division was to send its remaining brigade to Ye-u to cover that route. He then retired to bed and went to sleep in order to preserve the essential atmosphere of calm in his headquarters.

Major General Bruce Scott, commanding 1st Burma Division, took the necessary steps to launch the attack. However at 0500 hours on 1st May his own divisional headquarters was attacked by a Japanese penetration force, but fought its way out, carrying essential documents with it.

63rd Brigade, with a squadron of tanks, was the first to arrive and started the attack on Monywa which it was confirmed that the Japanese now occupied. They drove in the picquets but could not enter the town. The Japanese counterattacked twice that night.

Bruce Scott decided to attack Monywa with two brigades (16th and 13th) on 2nd May. 1st Burma Brigade, which was due to arrive that afternoon, was to be held in reserve. Both

Local Burmese are interrogated by the Japanese at jungle headquarters

The Japanese, due to this pressure, were recrossing the Chindwin and evacuating Monywa. But Monywa had lost its importance and the remainder of Burma Division broke contact and retreated north.

16th Brigade was ordered to Shwegyin and told to dig itself firmly in to protect the Shwegyin – Kalewa crossing of the 400-yard wide Chindwin.

Alexander and Stilwell met at Ye-u on 1st May and, in the light of the news from Monywa, decided to give up the line of the Irrawaddy without further delay. The bulk of 7th Armoured Brigade, which had been cooperating with the Chinese 38th Division on the west bank of the Irrawaddy north of Mandalay, was ordered back to Shwegyin via Ye-u. This was the last time the two commanders spoke as Stilwell's wireless set conveniently failed from there on.

The Japanese 56th Division had now landed in Burma and was sent with the 55th Division to destroy the Chinese Armies returning to China, whom they considered were their main foe.

33rd Japanese Division had two roles. The first was to destroy the remainder of the British forces retreating to Kalewa. The second was to pursue those remaining Chinese divisions, which had been cut off from China, into north Burma and destroy them.

The Japanese 213th Regiment with one mountain artillery battalion had taken Monywa. 214th Regiment was advancing from Shwebo towards Ye-u.

From the British point of view the situation developed into a race for Shwegyin between themselves and the Japanese. The British were encumbered with thousands of Indian refugees progressing along the same route. It was also a race against the arrival of the monsoon which might make tracks impassable for vehicles and tanks.

The main concern of the British was

brigades attacked, made some gains and were then held up. This was near the end of a very long retreat and officers and men were weary and lacking in spirit, especially as they had been rather foolishly told that they were on their way out to India.

That afternoon 1st Burma Brigade, with one battalion from 48th Brigade, passed through 16th Brigade's positions and tried to push on but failed to make any progress.

In the meantime the divisional transport, although frequently attacked, managed to by-pass Monywa and reached the road north to India. 63rd Brigade also suddenly withdrew north as well having received orders, which turned out to be untrue, that they should do so. Bruce Scott, however, decided to continue the attack but no progress was made. It was later said that the orders which 63rd Brigade had received had emanated from the Japanese, but it is more probable that they wanted to follow the divisional transport to home and safety.

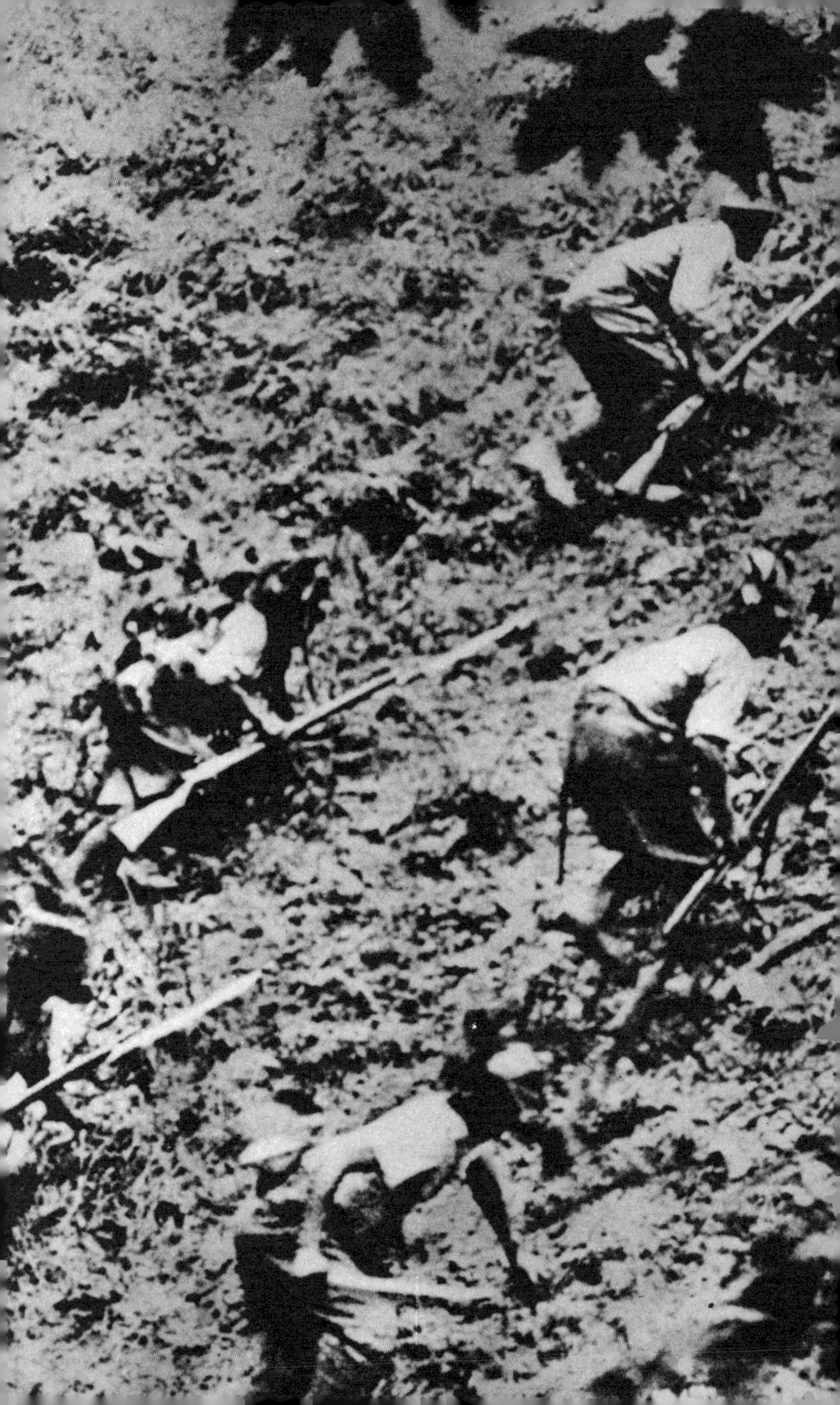

to save the tanks, and, if possible, the remaining guns of the two divisions and as many men as could make it. Casualties were given priority as Alexander was determined not to allow these men to fall into the hands of the Japanese who, at that time of the war, were bayonetting most prisoners as they did not want them to clutter up their advance.

Alexander impressed on Slim that this withdrawal from the Ye-u area was not to be completed until General Sun Li-jen's Chinese Fifth Army had moved north to Shwebo.

Slim made dispositions to protect his retreat. He ordered 48th Brigade to take up positions either side of the Chindwin to protect a boom which the engineers had laid across the Chindwin. The Japanese 213th Regiment advancing by boat up the Chindwin were attacked by RAF from India but this did not deter them and they continued their advance. On 5th May Japanese aircraft bombed and broke the boom, and on the 7th bombed Shwegyin.

On the 9th a Japanese battalion landed on the east bank of the Chindwin eight miles below Shwegyin. A company of Gurkhas, who had just arrived from the south, saw them landing at night but did not take any action although armed with machine guns and mortars. Their morale was at rock bottom and, although their orders were to intercept the Japanese, they made a wide detour around the Japanese to try and rejoin their battalion which they considered more important. En route they lost their company commander, who had fought all the way from the Bilin river.

Because the wireless batteries were run down no message was sent to warn 1st Burma Division at Shwegyin of this Japanese landing.

1st Burma Division had crossed the Chindwin and had been ordered by Wavell to retire to Tamu, where they

Japanese infantry attack uphill in Burma

could only just be adequately supplied by road and tracks from India.

The British crossing of the Chindwin at Shwegyin was in full swing and the 17th Division with the tanks had started to arrive.

However, at 0545 hours on the 10th, small parties of Japanese opened fire on the defensive position of the Royal Jat Regiment covering the crossing. The Japanese worked around this position and occupied a prominent knoll overlooking the basin from which the evacuation over the river was proceeding. This put the landing basin out of commission, for in spite of counterattacks, the determined Japanese could not be dislodged. But the three remaining river steamers came in under high banks 200 yards upstream and evacuated the rest of the sick and wounded.

As soon as Major General Cowan heard of the arrival of the Japanese he sent the 1st/3rd and 1st/4th Gurkha battalions, each now only one company strong, to protect his southern flank. He also moved the 2/5th Gurkhas and a squadron of the 7th Hussars in support. A counterattack in the afternoon failed. Little use could be made of the preponderance of tanks. Japanese pressure increased and most of their 213th Regiment became engaged.

Cowan decided to abandon Shwegyin and withdraw to Kaing opposite Kalewa. Because the track crossed precipitous little hillocks, all tanks, guns, mortars, motor transport, wireless sets and the remaining stores and equipment had to be destroyed. At 0500 hours the tanks, guns and mortars started rapidly firing off their remaining ammunition which produced one of the most ferocious little barrages of the war. The author, by chance, was on the receiving end and can vouch for this. This put a stop to any further Japanese advance.

The remains of 17th Division crossed successfully at Kaing without their guns, tanks and transport and the Japanese did not pursue. One tank only had been taken across earlier.

43

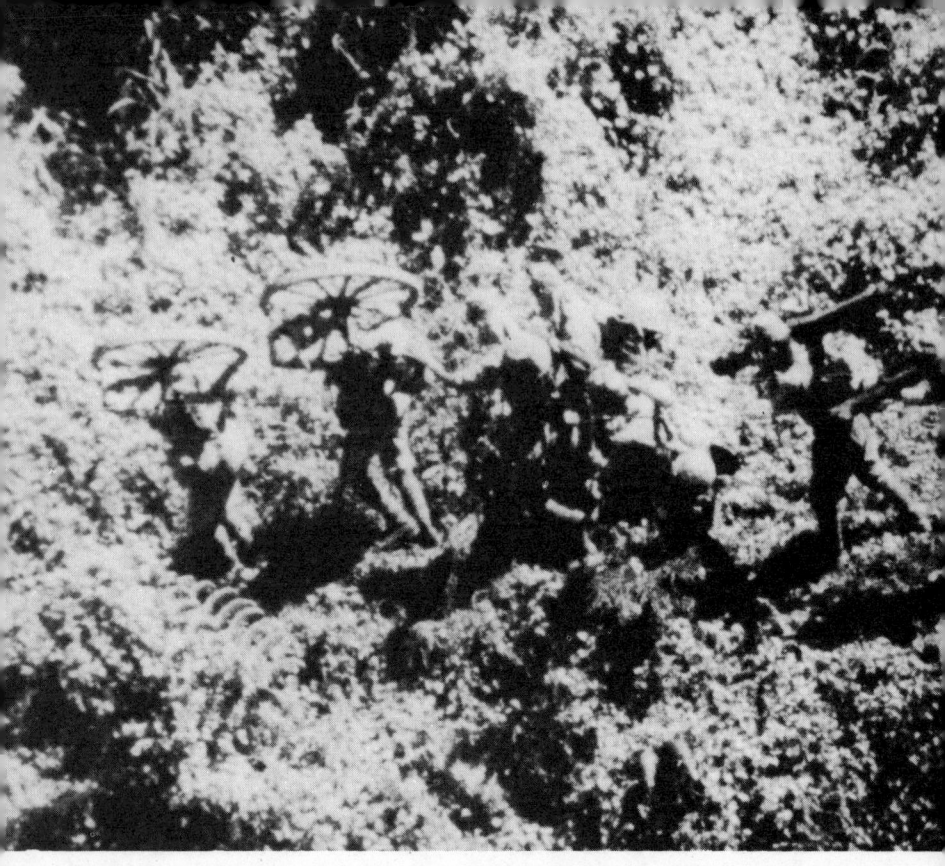

It later advanced in 1944 and returned to Rangoon where it had disembarked in December 1941.

The monsoon came down a few days later which brought all hostilities to a close as rivers and streams rose in spate.

Throughout the fighting Slim's place had been with his corps and sometimes he must have been wearied by the way other generals ordered his divisions and brigades about. His two efforts to attack had been forestalled by the withdrawal of the Chinese whose thoughts and efforts were drawn elsewhere by the Japanese retention of the initiative.

On the final retreat, Slim saw his Corps Headquarters safely across the Chindwin, and then returned to Shwegyin where he watched the final embarkation. He arrived just when the first Japanese patrols started to fire and his presence prevented any panic. He stayed and took charge of events until Cowan arrived from Ye-u with his own rearguard.

But Slim really never had a chance. He took over two ramshackle divisions both of which had suffered defeat in battle. He had no further reinforcements. The Japanese had air dominance and were equipped with excellent landing craft with which they were able to exploit the waterways and turn the flanks of his earthbound and roadbound troops.

Although in the later stages the Japanese needed only one regiment to chase his divisions, this was enough in the state they were in. The Burmese battalions had practically folded up, and could not be relied on. The three British battalions had taken the brunt of the fighting but only a few of the best men remained. The Indian battalions would hold together in defence but could not be trusted to attack after their best officers and NCOs had been killed. Even Slim's own Gurkhas started to crack under the strain of a 1,000-mile retreat which has the doubtful distinction of being the longest retreat of any unit in the British army. The British like to glorify defeats and disasters, but it is difficult to find anything to praise.

The retreat had lasted three and a half months of which Slim commanded Burcorps for two. The British forces had lost 13,000 killed, wounded and missing besides nearly all their tanks, guns and vehicles. Yet during this gloomy and depressing period Slim, by his invariable habit of visiting as many units as possible up to the so called 'front line' had become recognised and identified by the troops. He did not stand aloof but shared their mental anguish as well as many of their physical hardships. He was as much at home with the British soldier

Japanese gunners carry forward a mountain gun through jungle

as he was with the Indian and Gurkha. This identification of himself with his men, added to his innate kindness and compassion, was his great achievement. This was what made him loved by his men and made up for any lack of brilliance and originality in thought. He was the British bulldog, unlovely, but sure and obstinate and who would not let go under any circumstances.

When he was forced to relinquish his command at Imphal the men whom he had led through the shadows of darkness, cheered him. Slim said of this 'To be cheered by the gaunt remains whom you have led only to defeat is infinitely moving – and humbling.'

XV Corps and the Arakan

Top: The Tripura Rifles, an Indian State force, in the jungles of Arakan.
Above: Lieutenant-General N M S Irwin, DSO, MC, GOC IV Corps and, from July 1942, GOC Eastern Army, India.
Left: Lieutenant-General G A P Scoones, GOC IV Corps and defender of Imphal.
Above right: Sir Stafford Cripps (left) with Mahatma Gandi before the latter's imprisonment for organising revolt and sedition in July 1942. *Right*: Sir Stafford Cripps with Pandit Jawaharlal Nehru before the rejection of the Cripps Mission proposals by Congress which led to widespread mob violence, arson, murder and sabotage along the British army's communications

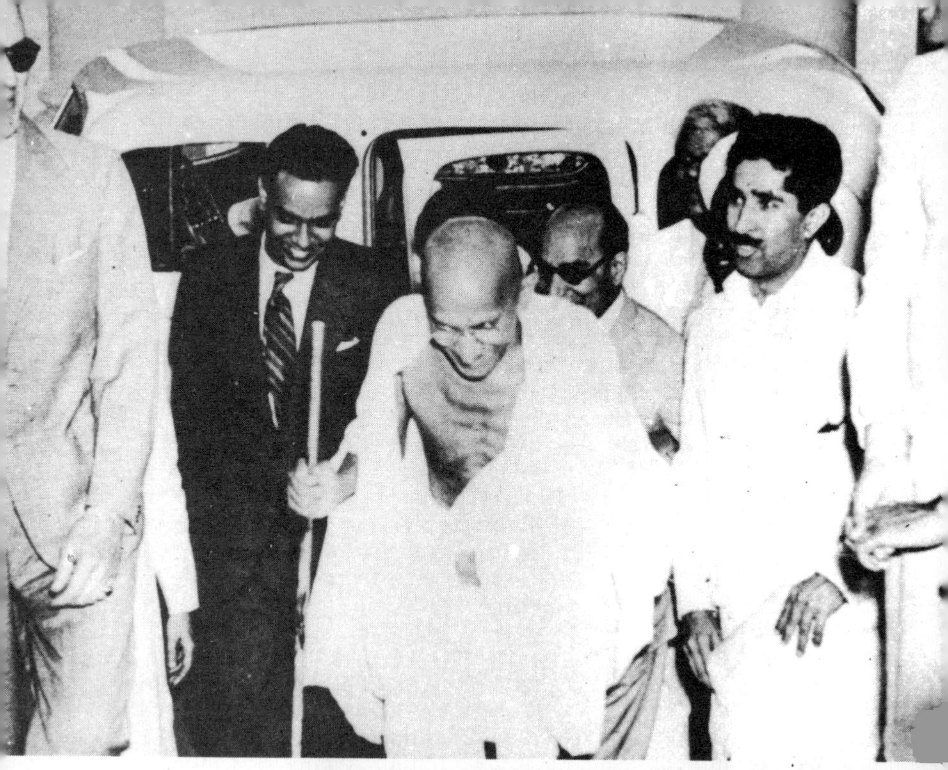

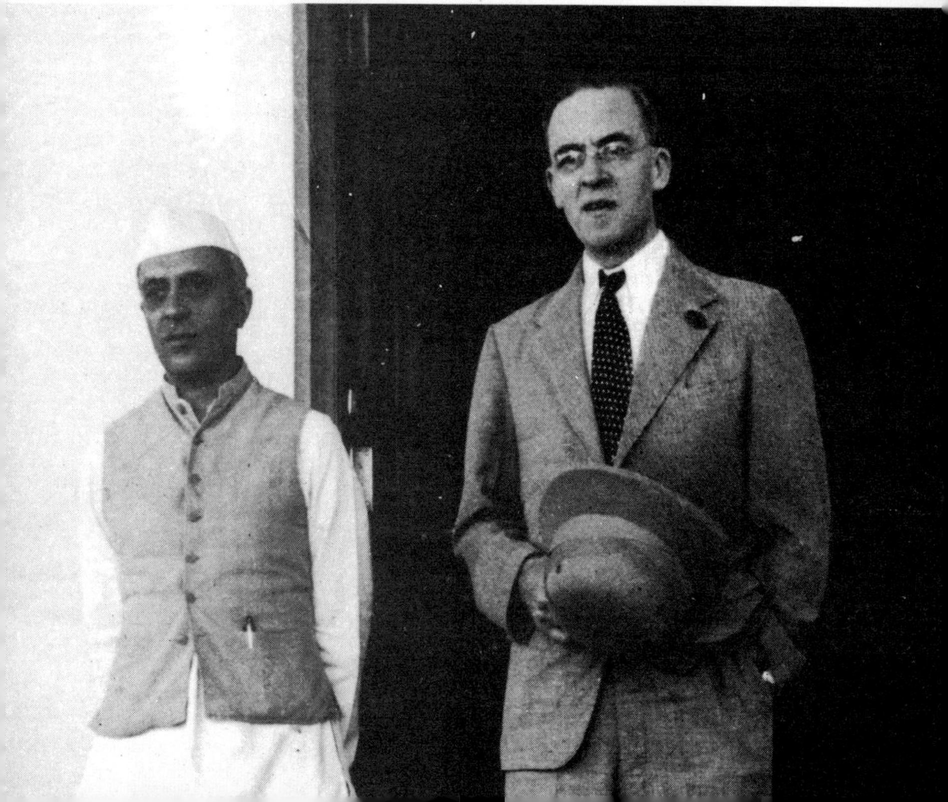

Lieutanant General N M S Irwin, commanding IV Corps Headquarters, had been sent on 30th April by Wavell to take over the Imphal area as the defeated Burcorps withdrew. Irwin brought up 23rd Division to this front, and out of the remains of Burcorps a new 17th Light Division of two brigades was formed, still under Cowan, and mostly composed of Gurkhas. Irwin was promoted to command Eastern Army and Lieutenant General Scoones, another 6th Gurkha of the days when Slim was adjutant, took over command of IV Corps.

Slim was appointed to command XV Corps, with the onerous job of maintaining law and order in Bengal where there was an extremely serious internal security problem. After the Cripps Mission had promised to grant Indian independence when the war ended, the Indian Congress Party demanded on 14th July 1942 the withdrawal of all British rule in India at once. Mahatma Gandhi, Pandit Nehru and other prominent leaders were arrested and imprisoned as a result, and threatened with deportation.

Eastern India promptly erupted in unprecedented scenes of riot, rebellion and sabotage. Isolated British and RAF troops were killed or burnt alive and many railways, post offices, and telegraph communications cut and destroyed. These attacks were carried out at strategically important points, indicating careful planning. At one time bridges on all roads and railways leading from India to Bengal and the army fighting the Japanese were destroyed. This also caused a breakdown of supplies and distribution of rice and other foodstuffs, resulting in famine conditions in the Bengal area swollen by war refugees. Over sixty British and Indian battalions together with the RAF in the area, a total of 100,000 men, were required in the summer of 1942 to put down this insurrection and restore order.

When settled conditions returned so that more brigades were available, Slim settled down to train his new divisions in the light of what he had learned in Burma. He laid down that emphasis should be placed above all on fitness. Small forces were separated from their battalion to patrol on their own for days; swimming and water crossing became part of the training, as well as digging and field defences and lessons on the use of mules. Above all he tried to train his commanders' minds so that they did not feel that they were 'cut off' and had to retreat if a few Japanese got behind them. He made every unit, including the medical arm itself, train on the ranges and have plans for defence since the Japanese were totally oblivious to the rights of non-combattants. Other formations had also come to much the same conclusions, but Slim was tireless in seeing that his memoranda on training on these lines should be carried out day and night. There was particular emphasis on night training, which had been sadly lacking in both the British and Indian Armies' training curricula in peacetime.

Wavell wanted to take the offensive against the Japanese, but the war had gone against the Allies in the Middle East at this time (autumn 1942), and the army in India was further weakened in order to assist that theatre. An offensive back into central Burma was therefore not possible (except by Wingate's raiding forces), so Wavell decided to try to capture Akyab Island on the Arakan coast. If successful, this would reduce the threat of a Japanese advance along the coast into Assam and Bengal, and would also provide an airbase for the RAF to support an offensive into Burma. But the main purpose of this limited venture was to win some sort of victory for the Indian Army, to help restore its morale and prestige at home and in Britain, which at this time was very low. Akyab, with its small garrison and limited communications with the rest of Burma, looked ripe for plucking. On 17th September Wavell issued an operation

ARAKAN CAMPAIGNS 1942-43-44

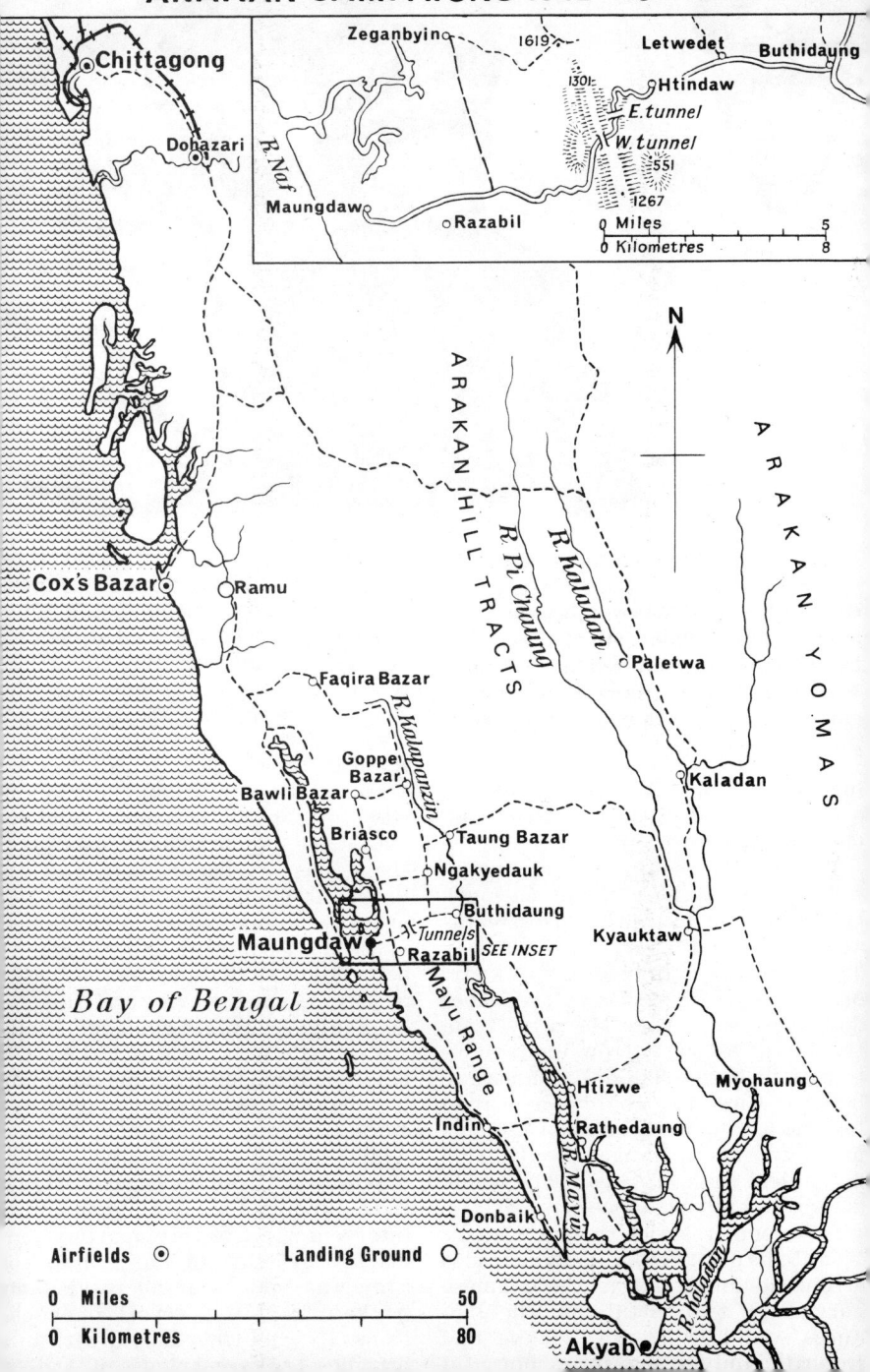

Above: Major-General Morris, Admiral Pellenger, and Major-General Lloyd, GOC 14th Indian Division, observe jungle training. *Right*: 5th Mahratta Light Infantry on captured Mayu Ridge, Arakan 1942. *Above right*: Mule train emerging from the famous Maungdaw-Buthidaung tunnels in Arakan

instruction to Eastern Command ordering the capture of Akyab and the reoccupation of Arakan.

The country leading to Akyab consists of a series of north-south ridges cut up by numerous streams and rivers, with very high rainfall. There are two main routes to Akyab, one along the coast and the other down beside the wide Mayu river, on the far side of the narrow and precipitous Mayu Range. The only connection between these two routes was a road leading through a series of tunnels under the Mayu Range, about forty-five miles north of Akyab. The whole area has a high incidence of malaria.

In December, Major-General Lloyd's 14th Indian Division, four brigades strong, advanced against the Japanese garrison of two battalions. The Japanese withdrew to Rathidaung and Donbaik, only a few miles north of Akyab, drawing the British further into the appallingly difficult countryside. Here for nearly a month Lloyd tried and failed to break through the Japanese defences. By this time, reinforcements from central Burma were reaching the Japanese, and Lloyd's force was brought up first to six brigades and then to nine. Further attacks failed against the cleverly sited Japanese positions, and by March the Japanese had gone over to the offensive. They cleared all the British forces east of the Mayu river, and were all set to destroy the British in the Mayu peninsula. Not being road-bound like the British, they succeeded mostly by manoeuvre and did not need to do very much fighting.

Slim saw first 14th and then 26th Division removed from his command to make this abortive offensive, since Irwin, as Commander Eastern Army, chose to fight the Arakan battle direct from his headquarters in Barrackpore, Calcutta, without an intervening Corps Headquarters commanded by Slim. In March, however, Slim was sent by Irwin to visit the Arakan front and report on conditions. By this time Lloyd, with nine brigades, tanks and plenty of artillery

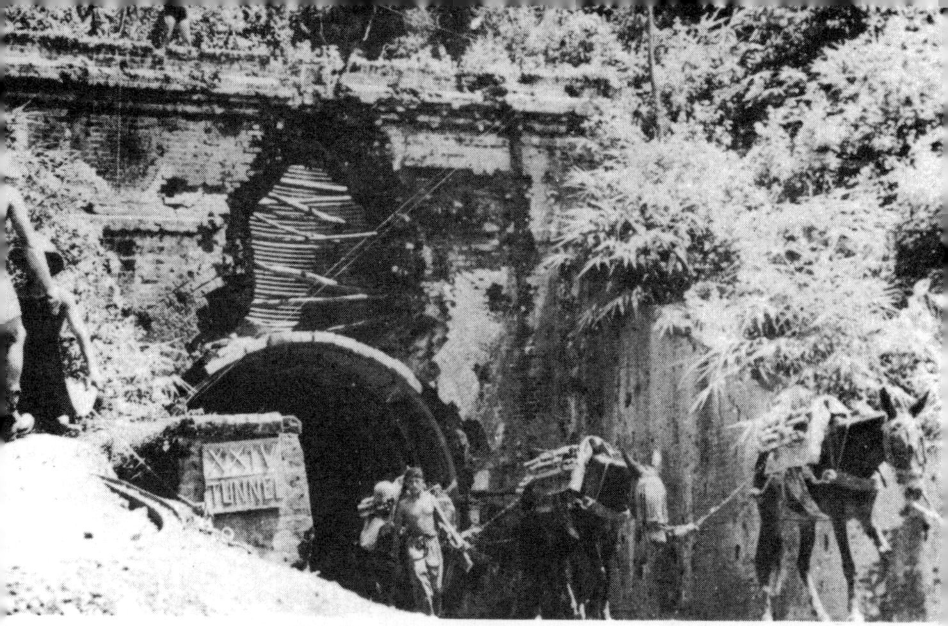
XXIV
TUNNEL

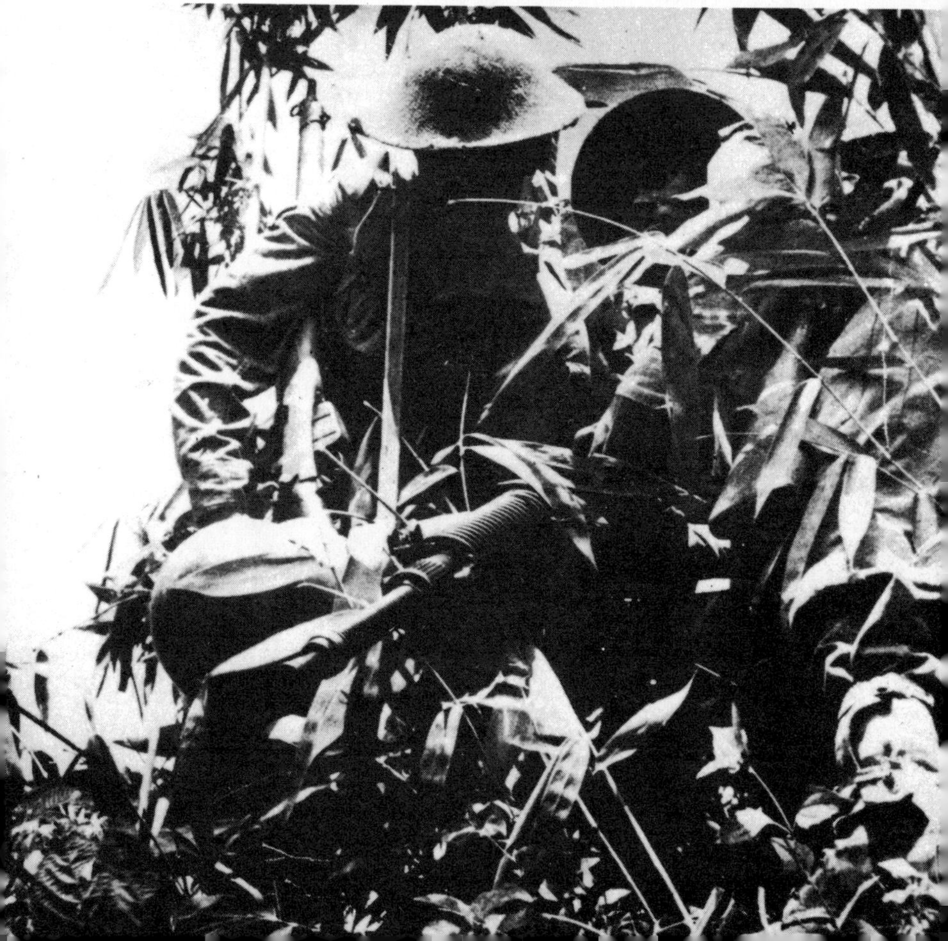

against, at the most, the equivalent of two Japanese brigades, was at his lowest ebb.

Slim reported that having nine brigades under one divisional commander was basically wrong as control was impossible. He reported that the tactics carried out by these brigades were confused and no lessons had been learned from the operations of Burcorps during the retreat. In fact Lloyd's forces were making all the same mistakes. The result of this ineptitude was that the morale of officers and men was low.

By making such a report Slim was, by inference, criticising Irwin, his commander, who had tried to run this isolated campaign from his own headquarters 300 miles away from the sound of gunfire. Akyab had seemed such an easy target.

On 5th April, after the removal of Lloyd, Slim and his headquarters were ordered to move to Chittagong to prepare to assume operational command but not, curiously enough, administrative control. Slim found himself in a most difficult position. He was not fully in command and had with him only half his headquarters which he had scrupulously trained. The nine brigades in front of him were commanded by Major General Lomax whose untried 26th Divisional Headquarters had replaced Lloyd's. The Japanese were continuing to envelop the left flank of these nine brigades, two of which had been destroyed. Communications to the front were minimal, and the monsoon was due to break in four weeks time.

However, after nine anxious days, Eastern Command handed over all responsibility to Slim's XV Corps.

This was a situation in which a commander did not need special brilliance but steadfastness, calmness and courage – all of which Slim had. Slim decided that his monsoon position must be based on the Maungdaw–Tunnels – Buthidaung line. In order to be able to withdraw cleanly to this line he proposed first to attack the Japanese with the greatest number of men that he could apply in that difficult country. He ordered Lomax to prepare for an attack.

But as had happened three times before, he was too late and the more flexible Japanese moved first. Ten days after Slim had taken over, the Japanese put in a right hook against the Tunnels area.

Lomax tried to box in the Japanese but, although outnumbered, they easily broke through this trap and occupied the area of the Tunnels twenty miles nearer Slim's base at Chittagong. Lomax's plan had been a good one but, as had so often happened in the early years in this theatre, he just did not have enough trained officers and men and battalions of sufficient calibre and morale to carry out his orders. The Japanese, in spite of reinforcements, were still outnumbered by more than three to one and possessed no armour or heavy artillery.

The demoralisation was such that Slim considered withdrawing as far as Cox's Bazar in Assam. He felt that the Japanese should be allowed to occupy this dreadful malaria-ridden area, and that his troops should not try to confront them in the jungle where the Japanese could win by their greater mobility and enterprise.

He put this opinion in writing, emphasising the complete loss of morale of his frustrated troops. Irwin and Wavell reluctantly agreed with him. The withdrawal began on 11th May but, with the monsoon intervening, the Japanese did not follow up. 26th Division with its three brigades remained in the Arakan for the monsoon and the six other brigades were withdrawn to India to refit.

On 15th May a small drama took place. Slim was sitting down with his senior staff to dinner at a table in the open as the monsoon had not yet broken. Slim was silent and depressed at having had to take part in another defeat. The Chief Signal Officer came to the table and handed his general a

Lieutenant-General Sir William Slim with Fourteenth Army badge

secret and confidential signal which, because of its nature, he had personally deciphered. Slim read it, tightened his facial muscles, put the signal in his pocket and continued eating.

Shortly afterwards he was handed another Top Secret and Personal message by the same officer. Slim read it, relaxed slightly and threw both messages to his Chief of Staff, saying 'I think this calls for the opening of a bottle of port or something if we have one.'

The first message read. 'You have been relieved of your command. You will . . . return to Calcutta where you will await any further posting.' signed, Irwin, Lieutenant General, Army Commander. The second message read 'Cancel my first message. I have been relieved of my command and you are taking my place. Congratulations,' signed Irwin, Lieutenant General.

So Slim gained command of what was to become the famous Fourteenth Army.

A new look at the war

Both on the Retreat and in the Arakan the British forces were paralysed because the much smaller but more mobile Japanese forces could outmanoeuvre them and make them lose the transport and guns on which they relied.

All this was to be suddenly changed as that erratic military genius, Orde Wingate, appeared like a djinn on the scene, and transformed the Pacific war.

Slim had met Wingate in Abyssinia when they were both brigadiers. Wingate had won a famous victory in which about 400 of his men, mostly Sudanese and Ethiopian guerillas whom he had trained, had caused 12,000 Italians to surrender. He had then marched in triumph at the head of his Ethiopians, accompanied by the Emperor Haile Selassie, into the capital Addis Ababa. Slim was a then brigade commander who had lost his first battle.

The next occasion on which they met was when Slim had just taken over command of Burcorps in Prome in South Burma. Wingate was granted an interview by Slim, now a lieutenant general and corps commander. Wingate advanced and pressed home his theory that the answer to penetration was counterpenetration. Wingate had been sent by General Wavell to see if he could form or take over a guerrilla force in Burma. Wavell used Wingate in this way as an irritant to stir up his junior generals. He did this by extolling his original ideas on war and battle in a self-confident and masterly manner. On this occasion Slim pointed out that he had just taken over, he was not impressed by the units under his command who had not been taught how to fight orthodox warfare let alone guerrilla warfare, and that he had no troops at all to spare for what he considered useless and unnecessary diversions.

Brigadier-General Old (USAAF), Slim, Major-General Wingate, Major Gaitley, and Brigadier Tulloch

Slim talked very much from the prewar Staff College text book. He had been confronted with an appalling task for which he would need every one of his rapidly diminishing number of soldiers. He certainly could not afford to let the last of them volunteer for an attractive sounding but possibly futile diversion.

Wingate appreciated Slim's difficulties and after a further few minutes conversation in private, Wingate went back to Maymyo where he wrote a long appreciation of the situation to Wavell saying, in effect, that it was too late to think about raising penetration brigades in Burma, and that he should return to India and start again from scratch to raise a force for an offensive in the following year.

During the remainder of 1942 Wingate formed and trained a brigade of two battalions, one British and one Gurkha. From February to May 1943 this force crossed the Chindwin in the Imphal area, marched an average of 1,500 miles behind the Japanese 'lines' and returned after losing a third of their number in casualties.

During the whole of this period this force was supplied and supported from the air. Thus it not only proved that the Japanese were not invincible but showed how to counter the Japanese penetration tactics which had done so much to destroy the morale of the Indian army. Slim's long series of defeats, due to these Japanese tactics, could now be ended. The kudos for this great technical victory in military thinking, which was to change military strategy for the next thirty years, must rest on Wingate who, once he had fastened onto an idea which he thought was a winner, would see it through to the end against all odds.

Air supply was no novel idea to the British. It had been carried out occasionally when the situation demanded in Mesopotamia and on the North West Frontier of India since the 1914-1918 War. The Australian Independent Companies had rehearsed

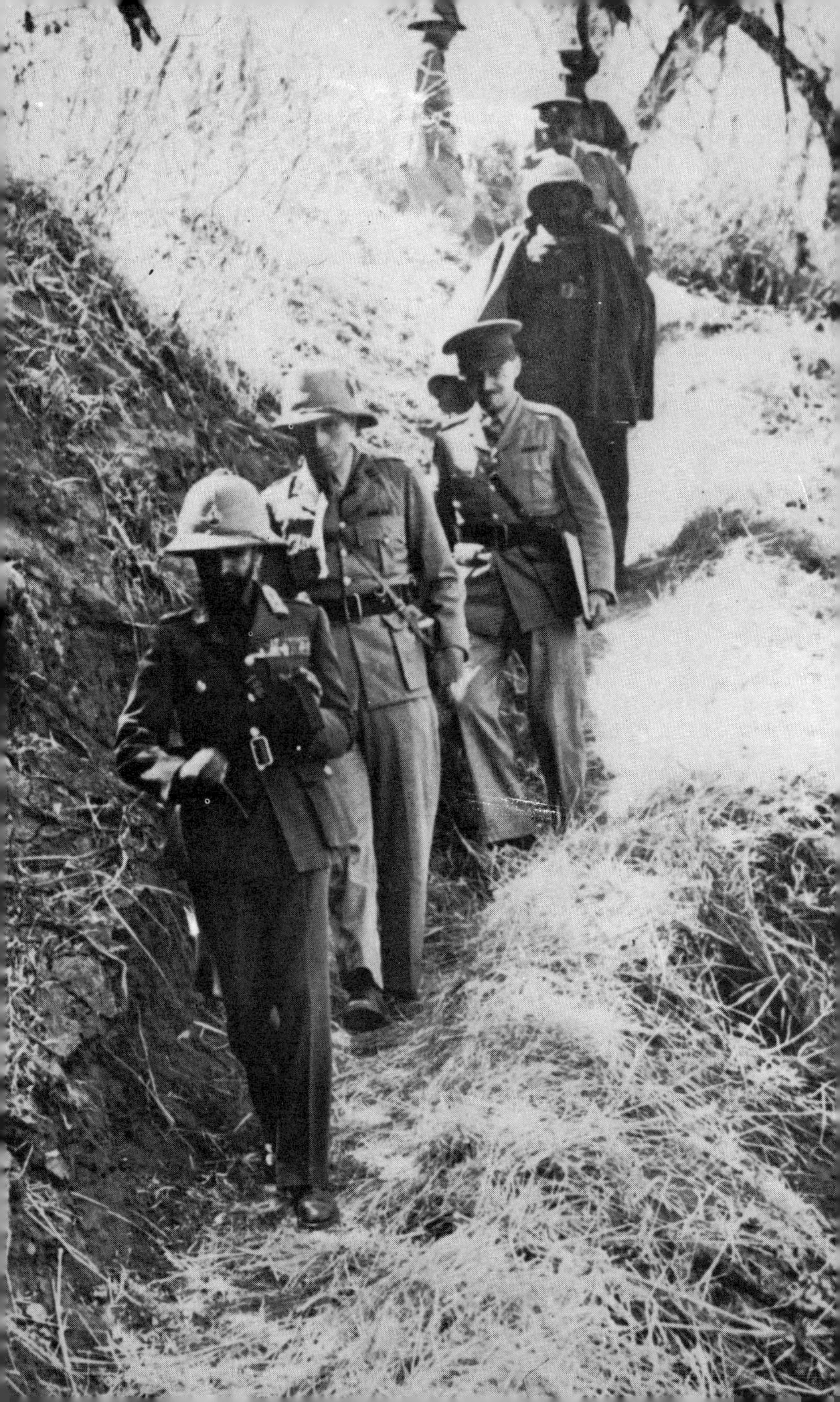

Elephants assist Chindits across Chindwin River on the first Wingate operation in Burma in 1943

and practised it in 1941 before their operations in the islands of Timor, New Guinea and the Solomons, and it was well developed by 1943. The Russians had used aircraft to resupply their guerrillas as had the Germans in their capture of Crete. But Wingate and his supporters had gone much further in trusting to the air implicitly as the only means of supply, with RAF signal detachments on the ground (using RAF wireless sets carried on mules) who could speak to the pilots, give them confidence and indicate what they wanted done. Squadron Leader (later Wing Commander Sir) Robert Thompson helped develop this close army/air force cooperation both at that time and later, and Colonel Peter Lord was the prime mover in the air supply base organisation, but no one would have forced this issue to fruition without Wingate's drive and energy.

The first Wingate operation was partially successful strategically but its greatest asset to the Allied side was the boost to morale it gave to the rest of the army. If Wingate's battalions, who were no better initially than the remainder in India, could run rings around the Japanese, so could they. As the Official History relates: 'The fact that the Chindits had entered upper Burma, damaged the railway, inflicted casualties and had been able to return, albeit without their equipment and animals, acted as a welcome tonic and to a large extent offset the failure in Arakan.'

There is no doubt that Wingate, in his fashion, had a most marked effect on the development of the more stereotyped Slim as a general. Wingate was always stealing the limelight by some great coup. Slim and his men, who had to bear the heat and burden of the day, learnt from Wingate's flashes of genius and adapted the lessons of his campaigns to their larger, more essential, staid and regular roles.

With a proved air supply and proper air support organisation Slim could now afford to plan and prepare an offensive without the fear in the back of his mind of having always to conform to his enemy's wounding penetration tactics.

Emperor Haile Selassie and Brigadier Wingate in Abyssinia, 1940

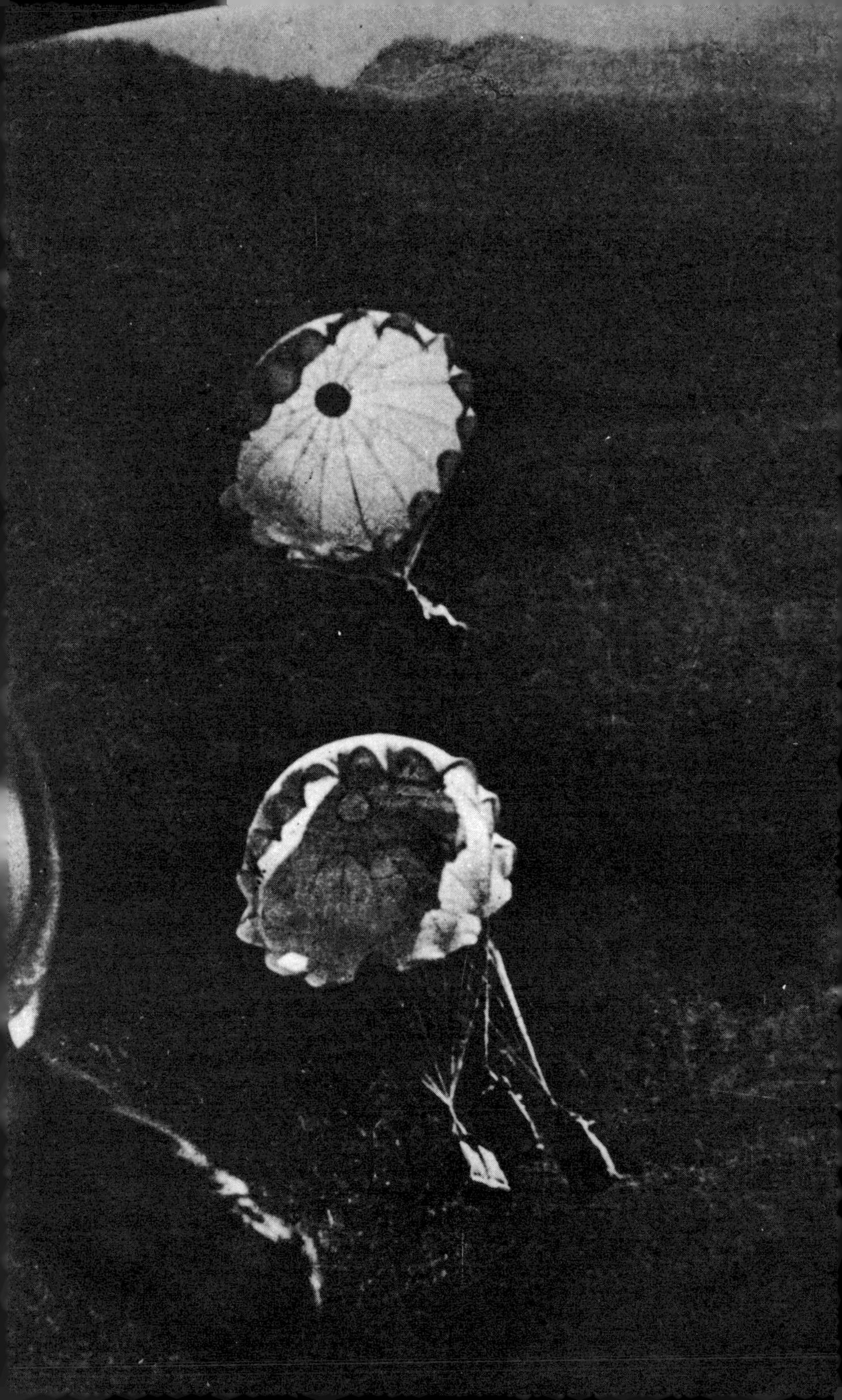

Left: RAF Dakota (C47) drops supplies to a Chindit column. *Above*: Chindit signaller operates a 22 set with wire aerial in open jungle. *Below*: Squadron-Leader Bobbie Thomson (RAF), Wingate and Brigadier Michael Calvert, commander 77th Indian Infantry Brigade, at White City

Raising morale

Wingate accompanied Churchill to the Quebec conference in August 1943, where the command structure of the Allied forces was completely reorganised, and a South East Asia Command (SEAC) was set up with a supreme commander at its head. The final choice for this job was Vice Admiral Lord Louis Mountbatten after the American suggestion that Wingate should have it was turned down by the British Chiefs of Staff. Stilwell was made Mountbatten's Deputy Supreme Commander. An integrated British-American staff would serve under them. India and South East Asia Commands would be separate. All ground forces east of Calcutta would come under SEAC and be formed into the Eleventh Army Group under General Sir George Giffard from East Africa. Fourteenth Army, which Slim now commanded, would be part of Eleventh Army Group, and include the divisions in the Arakan, those in the Imphal area, and also the projected new Chindit force when it entered the operational area. Thus began a successful partnership which lasted for nearly two years, as Giffard and Slim liked and respected one another.

The obvious way to recapture Burma and destroy the Japanese forces there would be to seize its only port, Rangoon, without which the Japanese forces would 'wither on the vine'. This possibility had to be abandoned because of the lack of landing craft, and so the plans for 1944 were geared to the main American interest in Burma – as the only route whereby a supply line could reach China and thus prevent it falling out of the war altogether.

The Quebec Conference thus decided that the main object of a 1944 Burma offensive would be to open up a road and a pipeline route from Ledo via Mogaung and Myitkyina to Kunming. The pipeline would supply an American bomber group which would bomb Japanese targets, and fighter squadrons to support Chinese forces on the mainland. An area south as far as Indaw would be held by the Allies to protect this route to China. Fourteenth Army would assist with an offensive from Imphal to Indaw. But the main feature of this plan was for Wingate, with an enlarged Chindit force of six four-battalion brigades, to cut and keep cut the communications running from the south to the Japanese forces opposing Stilwell on the Ledo Road and the Chinese on the Mekong River to the east, until such time as that area could be taken over by regular divisions of IV Corps.

So Slim's role for 1944 was the limited one of supporting the Chindits while Stilwell's American-trained Chinese and the Chinese armies in Kunming would advance. Stilwell was placed under Slim's command for this offensive, but being also Deputy Supreme Commander he could do much as he liked. One reason for Slim being given such a limited role was that India Command under Auchinleck had made so much of the administrative and engineering difficulties of Fourteenth Army advancing east into Burma, that Churchill and Roosevelt, with their advisers, felt that they could get little offensive action out of the Indian Army. Auchinleck had not yet understood the new powers, mobility and freedom of action that air supply presented.

The Japanese, however, were also considering offensive action. The first Chindit operation had shown them that their communications were now vulnerable to attack across the mountains. In June 1943, the Japanese command in Burma held a conference to study how best to defend Burma in the light of the Chindit operations of that year. This conference decided that the best way to forestall the British offensive, of which there were ample indications, would be to attack and cut the vulnerable British communications to IV Corps, which hung down like a bunch of grapes from Dimapur in the Brahmaputra valley.

General Slim talks to a Gurkha

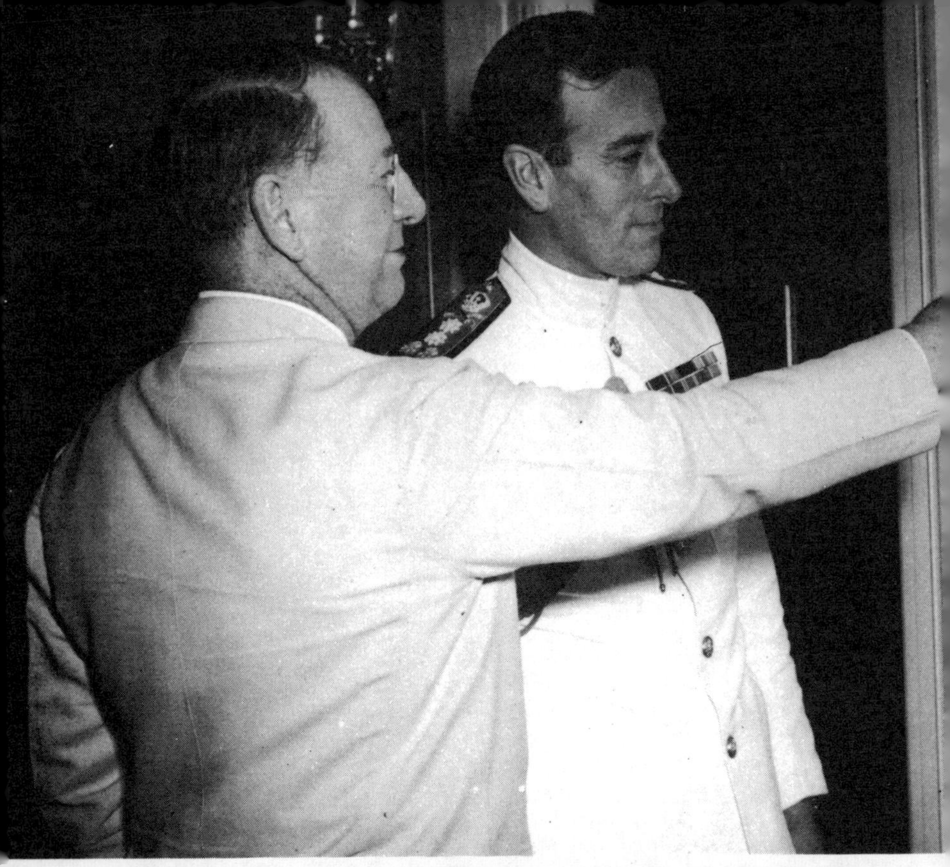

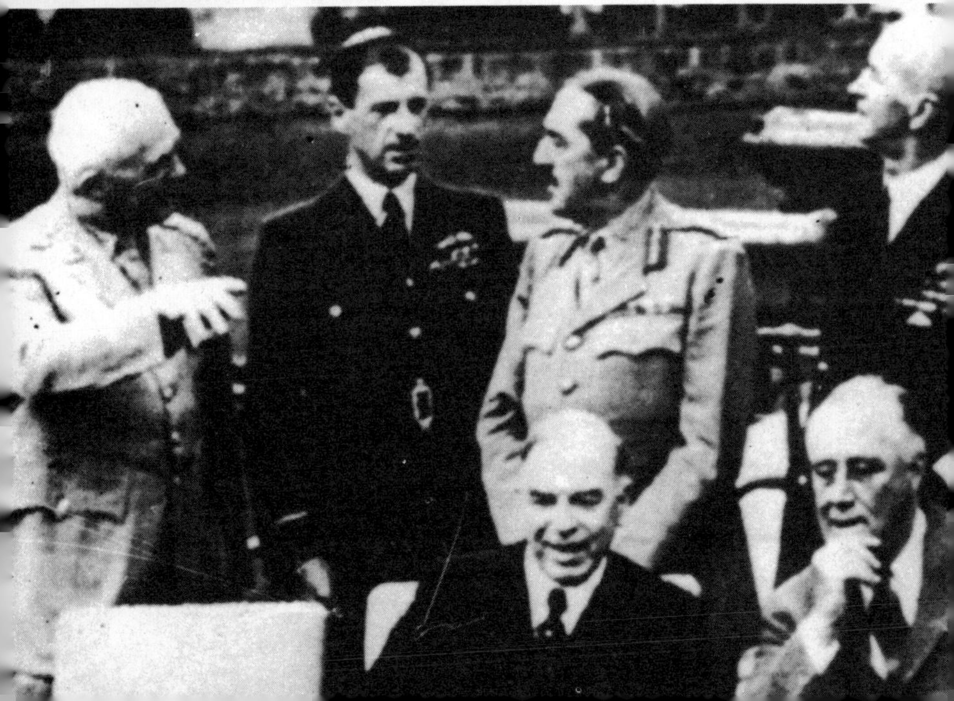

Left: US Secretary of the Navy Frank Knox discusses strategy with Admiral Lord Louis Mountbatten in Washington, August 1943. *Above:* General Sir George Giffard, GOC-in-C, Eleventh Army Group. *Below:* Canadian Prime Minister Mackenzie King, President Roosevelt and Mr Churchill with staff at the Quadrant Conference, Quebec

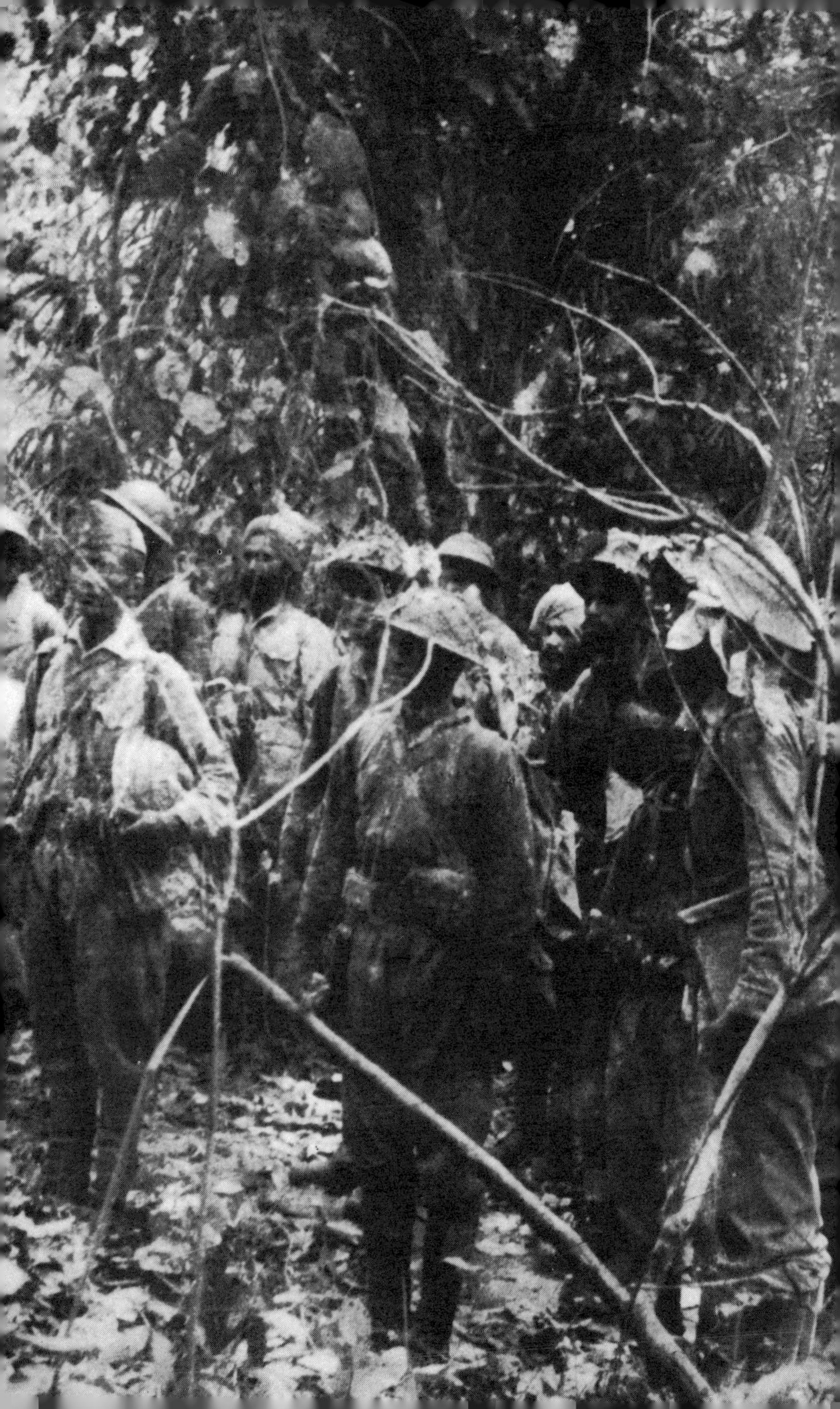

They could then turn and destroy the three British-Indian divisions based in the Imphal-Kohima region. They would first make a diversionary attack in the Arakan to draw off Fourteenth Army reserves, before launching their attack to the north. As a result of this conference, Burma Area Army also reported that an advance into central Assam was beyond the capabilities of the army as it then was.

Tokyo viewed the whole plan from a political and military viewpoint. The Japanese had formed an Indian National League and Indian National Army (INA). They had adopted an aggressive policy towards India in the hope of strengthening the formidable anti-British independence movement, so that the British would find it impossible to use India as a base of operations. Imperial Headquarters decided that they would use this offensive (which they hoped might offset their defeats in the Pacific) as a means of stirring up further trouble in India by bringing in the INA, which consisted of about one brigade of effective troops. They also reinforced Burma with two further divisions and an independent brigade.

Slim's Fourteenth Army was drawn into the campaign by the Japanese offensive. The Japanese still despised the British – Indian forces which until then they had always been able to defeat with inferior forces. This time they were to overstretch themselves as they did not fully appreciate the value of air supply and support. They did not realise that the Imphal plain was suitable tank country and they advanced practically without armour in an effort to destroy the British forces at a single stroke. They also depended on the capture of supplies to maintain themselves, and their lines of communication were vulnerable to Chindit penetration.

Slim was concerned first with the

Indian 'National' Army in the jungle before the Mutaguchi offensive, March 1944

SEAC (South East Asia Command) newspaper, edited by Frank Owen, was flown to troops from Imphal and boosted morale

Japanese offensive in the Arakan, then with the Japanese attack on Imphal Kohima. His final objective would be to pursue the defeated Japanese into Burma after the Mogaung Myitkyina objectives had been achieved and the pipeline and road to China opened.

Slim was fifty-three in 1944 but he was still as active and spry as a man twenty years younger, and his energy and attention to detail in such matters as antimalarial precautions and patrolling, had invigorated all ranks under his command. He visited as many units as possible and made himself known.

Lord Mountbatten, who was an excellent judge of men, knew he had a winner when he first met Slim. He himself had followed a circuit of visiting every unit in the army, navy and air force soon after his arrival both to let himself be seen and to get the feel of the mood of the officers and men. He found them keen but frustrated.

Mountbatten imparted much of his knowledge of the sovereignty of command to Slim and advised him to carry out the same procedure. Mountbatten then did everything he could to build up the image of Slim as a hero, and he obtained the services of Frank Owen to edit two forces newspapers. Their main object was to identify all the scattered units as being united under one Fourteenth Army Command, all intent on the same purpose. The SEAC newspaper satirised the men's predicament and forced them to laugh at themselves, thereby relieving much accumulated tension. Future editions were soon awaited by all ranks with interest: they kept each effort in perspective and above all glorified the commanders and especially Slim.

Slim always realised this and laughed to himself over it, considering it quite ridiculous that he should have been elevated into such a position. But every powerful man should have a clever court jester who can make him see himself as others see him, and keep his feet on the ground and the man who took this

Slim talks to line of communication staff

role was Welchman, Slim's Chief of Artillery, who had stayed with him from Gallabat and Prome days. Ex-champion swimmer, gunner and wit, Brigadier Welchman was probably, next to Slim's wife, the most important factor preventing high office spoiling him and making him too pompous. This should not detract from Slim's own capacity to laugh at himself; he had not been a schoolmaster, and later a part-time journalist between the wars, for nothing. He could always take an objective view of a situation and this ability raised him above his corps commanders and other rivals for height. He also now had the confidence, the essential panache, the swagger from his Gurkha adjutant days, to carry off the ostentatious ceremonies of high command, and to make his subordinates realise that he meant business when he gave them orders. Orders were not just a subject for discussion as they often tended to be in the post First World War British army. Orders were meant to be obeyed.

There was, however, a chink in Slim's armour. He could never rid himself of his soft spot for the Gurkhas and their well known powers of exaggeration. He could never be too hard on his fellow Gurkha generals and treated them with a leniency which he did not accord to others. He knew that the Gurkhas were, in spite of their badinage, his most faithful and reliable supporters both in Fourteenth Army and in GHQ India and that he could always turn to them when the going was rough. As already indicated he was fortunate in having the support of an excellent loyal, personable and intelligent wife who was wiser than he, a fact which she took great pains to conceal but which he always acknowledged.

Slim was the one man above all in Burma to boost and maintain the morale of his officers and men, for had not he for two years shared their suffering? He hoped now to be able to promise them better times with air superiority, good rations, more armour and artillery, better roads, reinforcements and leave.

Japanese offensive

By the end of 1943, the Japanese had six divisions in Burma (15th, 18th, 31st, 33rd, 55th, 56th), with 53rd Division to come. Of these, 55th Division would be used for the diversionary offensive in the Arakan, and three divisions (15th, 31st and 33rd) would be used with the INA to attack Imphal and Kohima. The Japanese were also concerned about a sea-borne landing near Rangoon, and placed their reserve brigades in southern Burma as a precaution against this possibility. Their air strength had been considerably reduced by the withdrawal of units to strengthen their depleted air forces in the Pacific and the British now had effective air superiority.

To oppose this two-pronged four divisional attack (one in Arakan, three at Imphal) Slim initially had, besides air superiority, XV Corps (5th and 7th Indian, 81st West African Divisions) in the Arakan and IV Corps (17th, 20th, 23rd Indian Divisions) in the Imphal area, plus 26th Division and 254th Tank Brigade in reserve.

Slim also had under command Stilwell's three Chinese divisions (22nd, 30th, 38th) on the Ledo road in the north, and by 1944 would have the six brigades of Special Forces (the Chindits) available for offensive action against the Japanese communications.

To complete the picture XXXIII Corps (2nd British, 36th Indian, 50th Parachute Brigade) was in Fifteenth Army Group reserve with 19th and 25th Indian Divisions, 50th Tank Brigade and 3rd Special Service Brigade also available as part of the general reserve. In east Burma two Chinese armies were stationed on the Salween.

Well-camouflaged Japanese assault troops in Arakan

JAPANESE OPERATIONS HA-GO (Arakan) and U-GO (Imphal-Kohima) March-April 1944

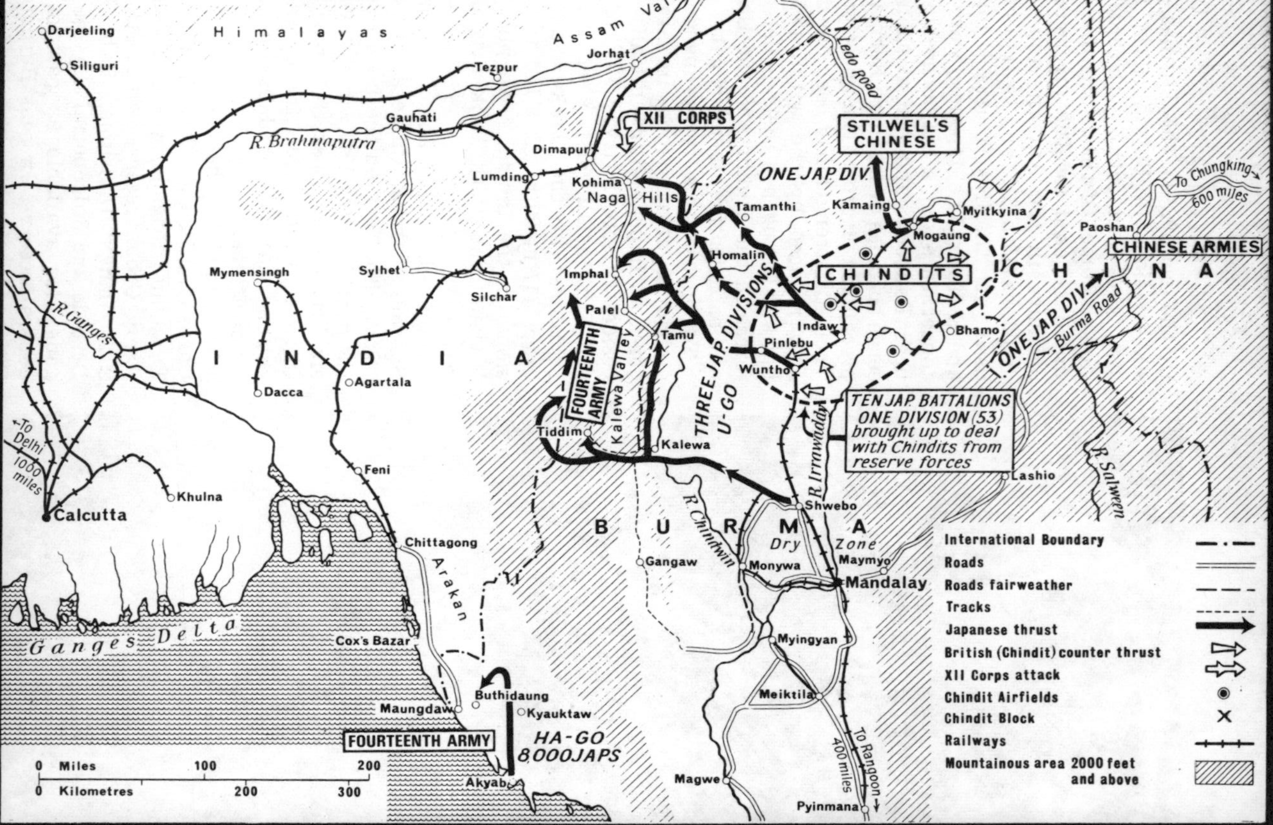

THE JAPANESE HA-GO OFFENSIVE February 1944

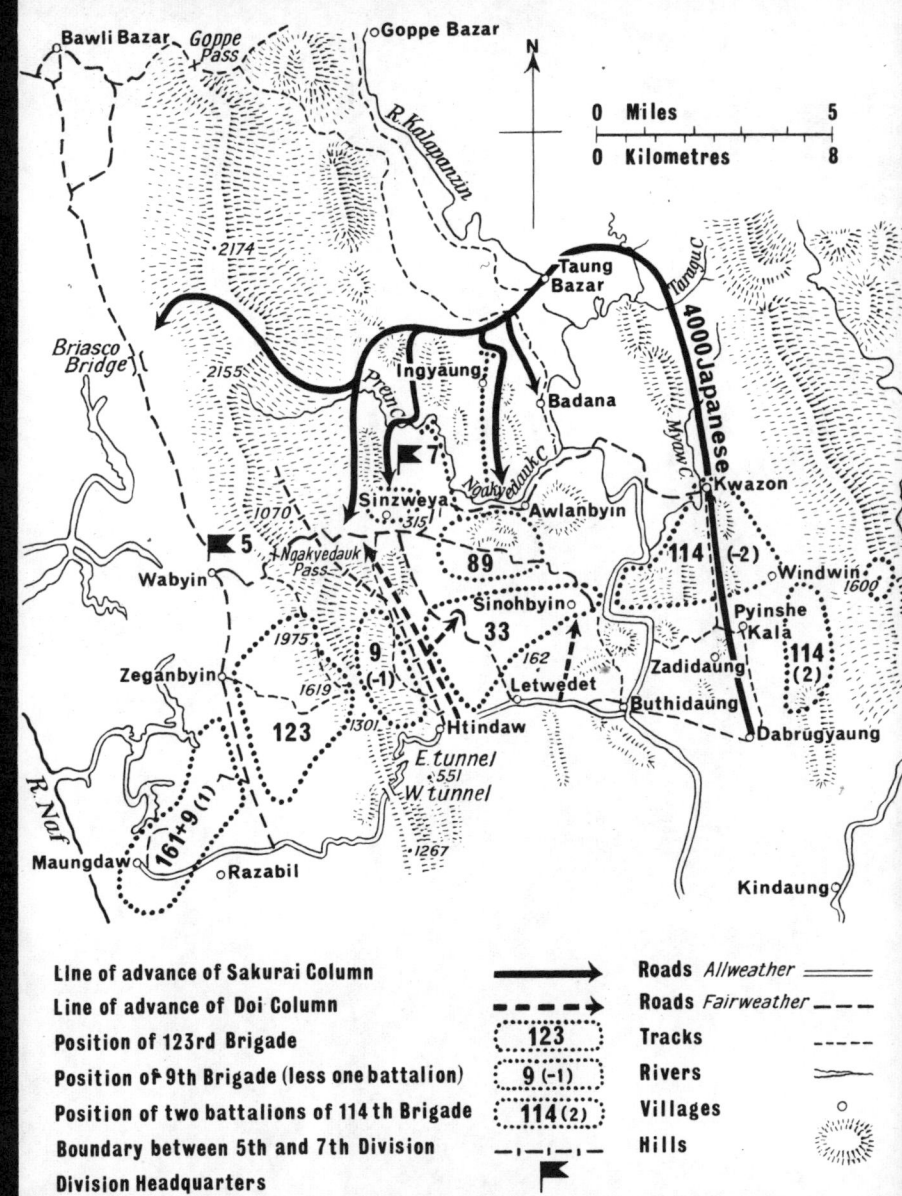

Legend:
- Line of advance of Sakurai Column
- Line of advance of Doi Column
- Position of 123rd Brigade
- Position of 9th Brigade (less one battalion)
- Position of two battalions of 114th Brigade
- Boundary between 5th and 7th Division
- Division Headquarters
- Roads *Allweather*
- Roads *Fairweather*
- Tracks
- Rivers
- Villages
- Hills

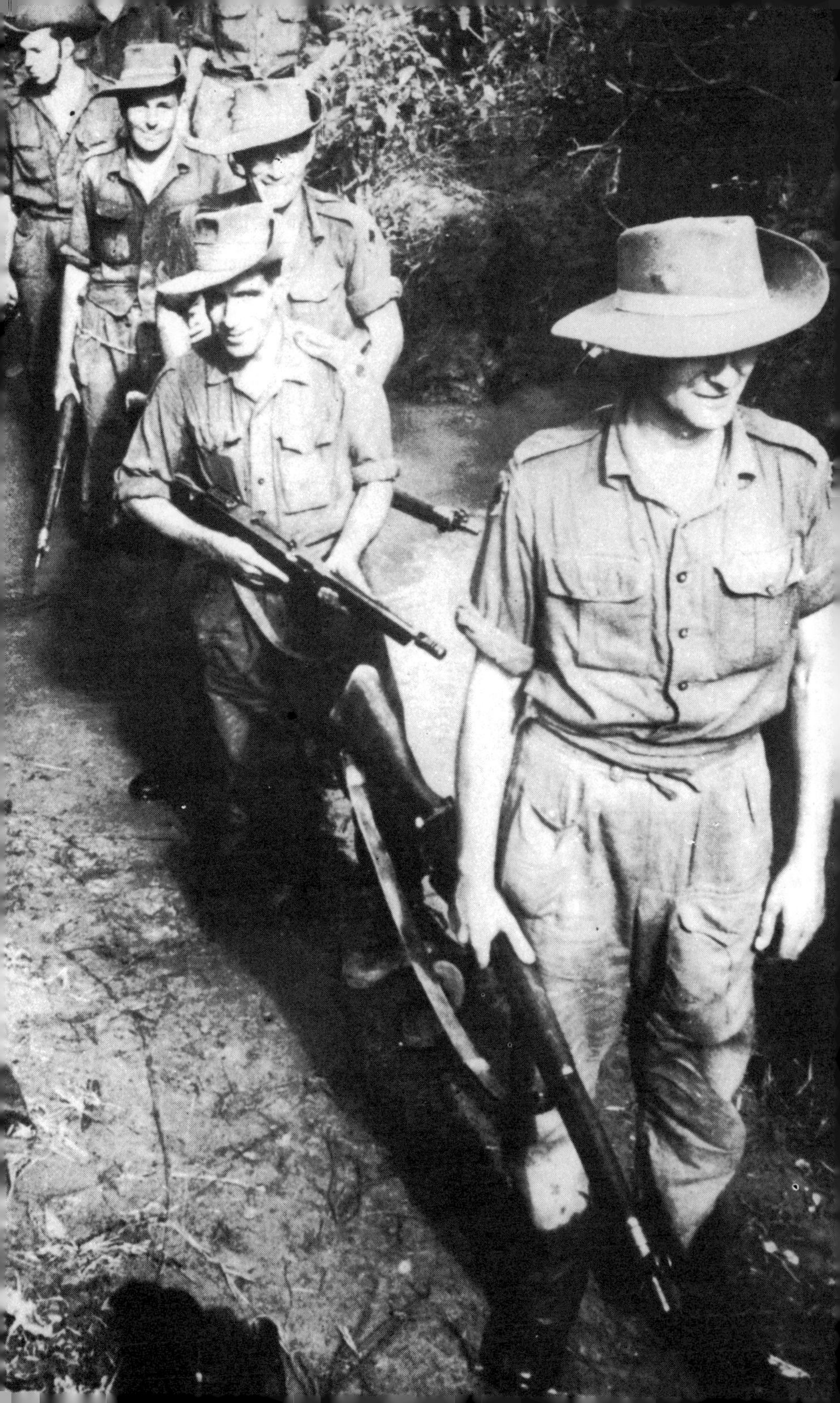

British gunners in action in the jungle

Slim therefore had a formidable force available but he found it difficult to apply his strength against the Japanese because of the lack of good roads. The Japanese also had the initial advantage of being on interior lines behind a massive obstacle, so that they could easily move divisions from one sector to another, while the Allies tended to be bogged down on the periphery.

But, excluding the Chinese on the Salween front, and including reserves held in Ceylon, the Allies had fifteen divisions, two tank brigades and about nine or ten independent brigades available to oppose a maximum of seven Japanese divisions and one mixed brigade in Burma.

We should now consider the Arakan theatre. It will be remembered that Slim, when commanding XV Corps, had had to pull back to the Bawli Bazar – Cox's Bazar area, leaving the

British troops pose for a photograph in Arakan

line Maungdaw (on the coast) – the Tunnels and Buthidaung (on the Mayu River) to the Japanese. The Japanese had spent the monsoon season in the summer and autumn of 1943 strengthening the line. Lieutenant General Christison, who had taken over XV Corps from Slim, deployed his divisions so that his 5th Division held the coastal strip, the 7th division was over the Mayu range in the Mayu valley, while he had sent the 81st West African Divisions on a wide flanking movement down the Kaladan river further to the east. The 25th Dragoons, a tank regiment, had also been moved up in great secrecy to the Arakan front. Road building was top priority.

During the last months of 1943 Christison had advanced his forces methodically down the Mayu peninsula so that, by the middle of January 1944, he was in a position for a general

Major-General T Sakurai, commander of 55th Infantry Group and of the Ha-Go offensive in Arakan

Major-General Frank Messervy, commander of 7th Indian Division. He escaped capture when his headquarters was overrun

offensive against the Japanese holding the Maungdaw – Buthidaung road. The Japanese, possibly to suck the British further down the peninsula in anticipation of their own counter-stroke, evacuated Maungdaw, but held strongly on to the Tunnels area in the centre of the line. Slim moved 26th Indian Division to the Arakan front as his own reserve in that area.

The Japanese 143rd Regiment was holding the Tunnels area, with a detachment on the Kalanzin (Mayu) River opposite 7th Indian Division.

General Giffard (Eleventh Army Group) and Slim (Fourteenth Army) had been concentrating XV Corps in the Arakan so that an attack on the Maungdaw – Buthidaung line could be made in the middle of January 1944, but XV Corps was already behind schedule.

5th Indian Division eventually attacked Rabazil on 26th January but after four days heavy fighting, made no progress. On 30th January Christison moved his medium artillery and tanks over the Mayu Range to 7th Division for them to continue the attack. On 2nd February Giffard, before he went on a tour of the Arakan front, visited Slim's headquarters. As a result he ordered the British 36th Division to concentrate at Chittagong, behind XV Corps, but with orders that it should not be used without his permission. So Slim now had five divisions available in the Arakan front.

On 3rd February 5th Division was facing the Japanese in the Tunnels area with all three of its brigades in the line. Two brigades of 7th Division were spread across a distance of ten miles from the foothills of the Mayu Range to across the Kalapanzin (Mayu) River. The third brigade, with tanks, was poised to attack Buthidaung. XV Corps Headquarters was at Bawli Bazar.

An 'Administrative Area' had been stocked with petrol, ammunition and supplies at Sinzweya.

Lieutenant General Hanaya, com-

General Christison, commander of XV Indian Corps

manding 55th Division, had been put in charge of operation 'Ha-Go' whose object was to cut the communication of the British 7th Division and destroy it, and do likewise to the 5th Division on the coastal strip. For this offensive, and including the garrisoning of Akyab, Hanaya had four regiments each equivalent to a British brigade. He had no armour nor medium artillery and no air supply. His artillery was on a pack animal basis.

Hanaya divided his division into four. Two battalions would hold Akyab. (At this time 36th British division were trained in seaborne landings and stationed at Chittagong with ninety-six landing craft.) One battalion would guard the coast of the Mayu peninsular. Two battalions (the Doi column) would hold the redoubts between the Kalapanzin river and the sea. (This line was being attacked in succession by 5th and 7th Divisions with a tank regiment and medium artillery.) He used his reconnaissance regiment to screen off the West Africans in the Kaladan valley.

Hanaya's main attacking force would consist of one regiment reinforced by two more battalions and an engineer regiment, totalling five infantry battalions in all. He put them under command of Major General Sakurai. He ordered this Sakurai column (totalling about 5,000 men) to pass through the 7th Indian Division's lines east of the Kalapanzin River and to seize Taung Bazar. It was then to cross the river, block the Ngakyedauk Pass in the Tunnels area and destroy British formations (7th Division) which lay between the Mayu Range and the Kalapanzin River. At the same time the Doi column manning the redoubts would attack from the south. A raiding party from the Sakurai column would also attack and destroy the Briasco Bridge thus cutting the road communications to 5th Division.

The Sakurai began its advance at 2300 hours on 3rd February. It moved north through the widely spread 114th Brigade's position, brushing aside the rearguard, which were the only enemy it encountered before occupying Taung Bazar at 0830 hours in the morning of 4th February. It had marched a distance, as the crow flies, of twelve miles at night over difficult country. Its main body in the early morning mist marched sixteen abreast in a compact group in the centre of a four hundred yard wide valley through the British lines.

Within an hour of arrival at Taung Bazar one battalion crossed the Kalapanzin River in captured boats, followed by two more battalions later in the day. The leading troops of these battalions met some troops of 89th Brigade that evening. By noon on the fifth all five infantry battalions and the engineer regiment (which was a fighting unit) were across the river.

On the fifth morning Sakurai ordered one battalion, less two companies, to cross the Mayu Range and seize the Briasco Bridge, thus cutting the Bawli Bazar – Maungdaw Road behind

75

A dead Japanese is searched for documents after the capture of Goppe Bazar

5th Division. One battalion was sent to seize the Ngakyedauk Pass in which the newly constructed road ran linking 5th and 7th Division. The remainder of his force was ordered to move south to seize Awlanbyin and Sinzewa where the British administration area was situated.

This boldly executed penetration movement took the British completely by surprise although some special reconnaissance patrols had predicted this operation from information received. Their warnings had been ignored. 114th Brigade Headquarters had heard the movement of men and animals passing by in the night but thought that it was ration parties moving forward.

When Major-General Messervy (Commander 7th Division who had had considerable battle experience in the Western Desert) heard at 0900 hours on the 4th that some 800 Japanese were advancing on Taung Bazar he ordered his reserve (89th) brigade to locate and destroy them.

On the evening of the 4th Slim ordered that air supply should be made available to the two divisions, and that a brigade of 26th Division should be made available to Christison.

Throughout the 5th 89th Brigade held its ground, but the tanks of the 25th Dragoons reported seeing large numbers of enemy marching towards the Mayu Range. Slim, on hearing this, placed the remainder of 26th Division under Christison's command, and ordered the division to advance to Bawli Bazar as soon as possible. General Giffard, who was visiting Slim, ordered the concentration of the whole of 36th Division at Chittagong.

By the evening of the 5th, therefore, the two leading divisions (5th and 7th) were holding their positions. As they had been placed on air supply the

76

cutting of their road communications was not important. At the same time strong reinforcements of two divisions were moving forward from the north.

Hanaya now ordered the Doi column holding the redoubts to attack north with as much strength as possible in cooperation with his attack on Sinzewa. Accordingly one of the two battalions advanced northwards energetically on the 6th.

But Sakurai's control of the battalions of his column was failing. A runner distributing a new list of call signs and wireless frequencies to replace those compromised was killed. This resulted in poor coordination of Sakurai's subsequent attacks.

The Briasco Bridge party raided the 5th Indian Divisional administration area and caused alarm, confusion and casualties. Another Japanese battalion attacked 7th Indian Division Headquarters and broke into the signal centre. They were eventually driven out but not before all communications were destroyed and codes compromised. Messervy, now unable to exercise control, ordered his headquarters to destroy papers and equipment of value and retreat in small parties to Sinzewa. Most of them succeeded in doing this during the next twenty-four hours. Japanese also overran some of Messervy's gun positions.

However the three brigade commanders of 7th Indian Division decided on their own to use 33rd Brigade Headquarters as a report centre and to hold their positions. This was a staunch and determined decision in the face of panic reports.

Christison, however, who believed that 7th Division was entirely overrun, ordered 5th Division under Major General Evans to move with all three of his brigades across the Mayu Range to Sinzewa.

At this stage on the 6th the more experienced Slim told Christison that he estimated that the Japanese could maintain a regiment in the rear of forward troops for only a short time.

Brigadier (later Major-General) G C Evans. He commanded 5th Indian Division at Imphal

Therefore it was essential that the two forward divisions should hold fast while he sent forward 26th and 36th Divisions to destroy these penetration forces.

In the afternoon of the 6th Messervy appeared in the Administrative 'Box' at Sinzewa and made disposition for its defence. As long as the Administrative area was held the enemy offensive must die out, as the Japanese relied on using its supplies for their own use.

The Administrative Box was to hold out from 6th to 24th February when the Ngakyedauk Pass was reopened. Its early defenders were the West Yorkshire Regiment supported by two tank squadrons of Dragoons, and some medium and mountain artillery. Again and again the perimeter was broken and restored by counter-attacks. But the hospital was overrun and all the doctors, nurses and patients were killed by the Japanese. Most of the ammunition dump was destroyed by Japanese artillery fire.

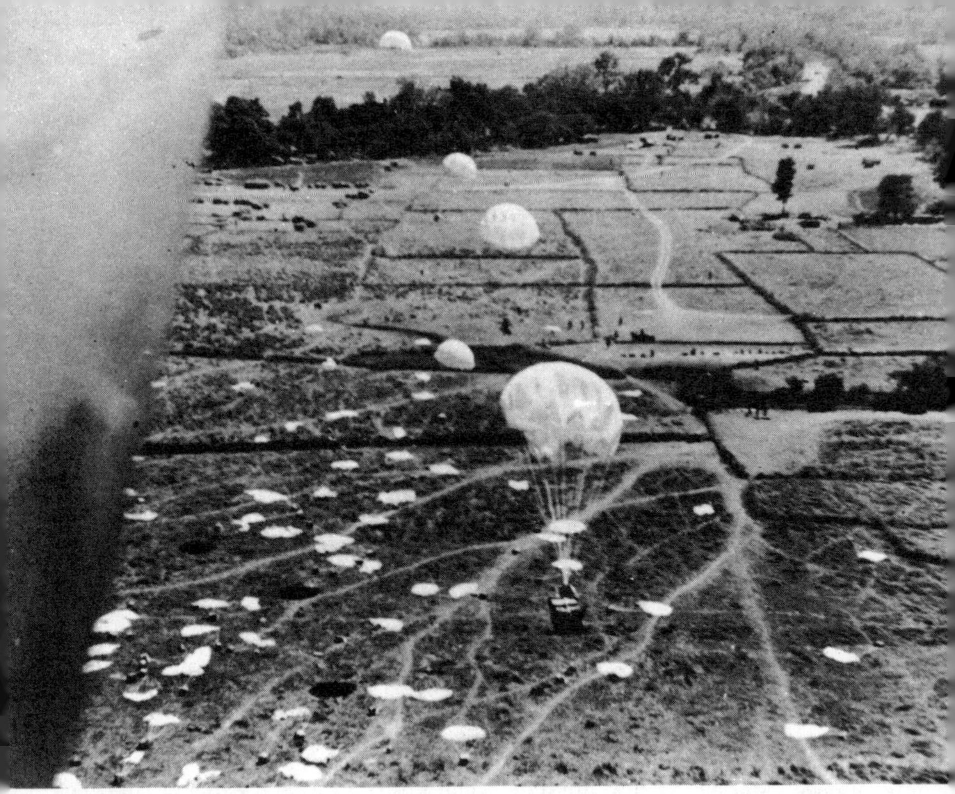

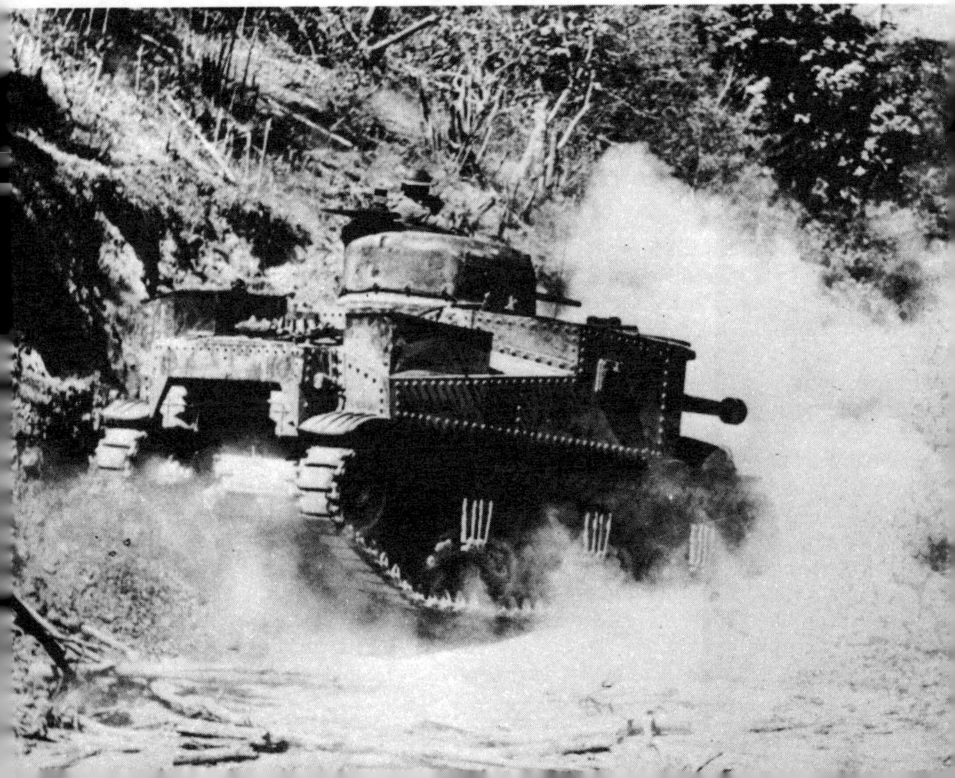

Air supply to forward troops in Arakan during the dry season

Elsewhere the brigades held their positions whilst 26th Division supported by 36th Division advanced south against strong opposition from small, experienced Japanese forces.

The Japanese had hoped to gain temporary air superiority over the battlefield to prevent air supply bringing their plans to naught. Between the 4th and 14th their fighters flew some 350 sorties, and their bombers attacked Bawli Bazar, Briasco Bridge and Sinzewa. They lost about fourteen aircraft with some damaged against the RAF losses of eleven fighters. Attempts at RAF supply were therefore hazardous in spite of air escorts, and some supply attempts had to be abandoned due to losses. A few supply aircraft, which had to fly at 200 feet to drop their supplies accurately, were brought down by Japanese anti-aircraft fire.

But from the 9th the RAF gained superiority and, in spite of some further losses, air supply was carried out every day thereafter. In five weeks Troop Carrier Command carried out 714 sorties and delivered 2,710 tons of supplies.

Tactical air support by fighter bombers assisted the ground forces to drive off repeated Japanese infantry attacks.

On 10th February General Giffard had realised that an attack on Akyab before the monsoon was now impossible so, as previously mentioned, he released 36th Division from its seaborne role to Christison, and moved up 25th Division to Chittagong in its place. 26th Division was making heavy weather of its advance as it was throwing off too many protective detachments on its line of communication, so great was the fear of the Japanese penetration prowess.

On the 16th the impatient Slim,

A British tank attacks Hill 1070, Ngakydauk Pass, Arakan

determined to gain a victory now that he had six divisions at his disposal, ordered Christison to resume his advance and clear the Tunnels – Buthidaung position. He also told him to make use of the 81st Division sitting static on the Kaladan using up valuable air supply sorties by ordering it to advance and threaten, in turn, the rear of the Japanese.

On the 13th Slim told Giffard that he was well satisfied with the way the battle was progressing. Air supply was now working well. 26th and 7th Divisions had met at Taung Bazar. The forward brigades of 7th Division were holding their positions (the Japanese had few men left to attack them). The Administrative Box was being held. 5th Division was disengaging a brigade to attack Ngakyedauk Pass.

The Japanese attacked the Box again on the 14th but, due to lack of communications, the attacks from different directions were not coordinated and went in piecemeal. Messervy decided to bring the rest of 89th Brigade into the Box as its garrison was getting tired.

By the 23rd Ngakyedauk Pass had been cleared. 500 casualties were evacuated by road from Sinzweya, and air supply to 7th Division ceased.

Slim was in a hurry to wind up events in the Arakan as he was certain that this attack was only a preliminary to a major attack on IV Corps' front in the Imphal area. He wanted the situation stabilised so that at least two divisions could be placed in reserve.

On the 24th, with the approval of his Army Headquarters, Lieutenant General Hanaya abandoned the 'Ha-Go' offensive. 112th Regiment had already started its withdrawal without orders due to complete lack of food.

That was the end. The Japanese withdrew uneventfully. The battle had cost XV Corps 3,506 casualties. But from the Japanese point of view it was a very creditable effort. One Japanese division had thrown two

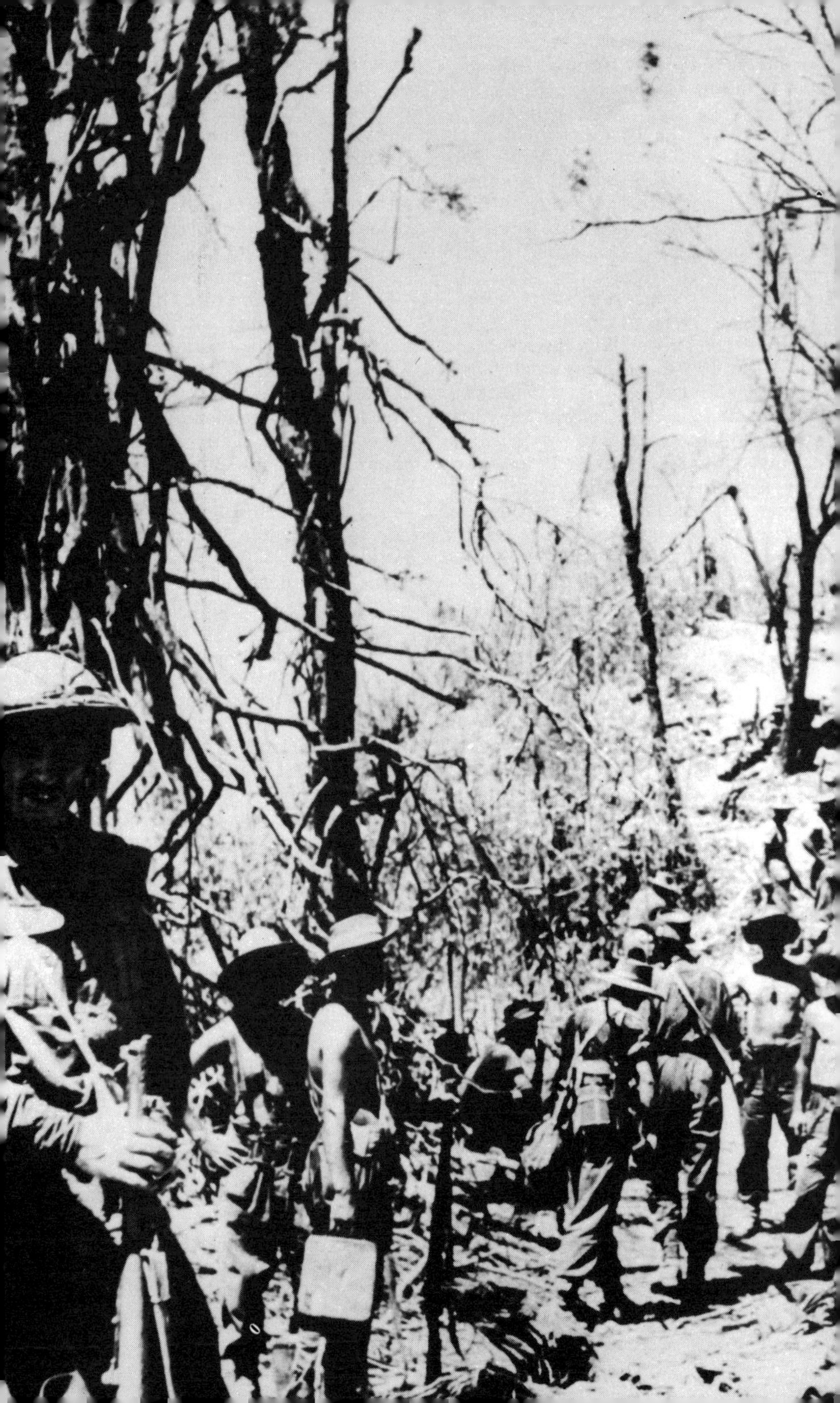

divisions into turmoil for a time, and the British had brought a total of six divisions against them. The actual Ha-Go offensive was carried out by 8,000 determined Japanese troops against what eventually amounted to 180,000 British troops. These included 27 Indian, 18 British, 7 West African and 5 Gurkha battalions, and a total of 26 regiments of artillery. Not all of these were deployed or brought into action. Lieutenant General Hanaya, Major General Sakurai and not more than four colonels were opposed by eight British major generals and twenty-seven brigadiers. At times the whole of 5th Indian division was holding its position against only one Japanese battalion.

But it was an important victory for the British and was hailed as such. It was the first time a Japanese attack on the continent of Asia had been held by the western powers. The Australians had found out how to do this in New Guinea eighteen months before, but they were a cohesive entity who could trust each other.

The triumph was really Slim's. It was mainly his determination which made the divisions stand firm in face of what appeared to be disaster. Indian troops had fought alongside British troops with some success. The divisions had seen that they could rely on air supply and need not retreat if their road communications were cut.

Much was made of the British-Indian victory in the Arakan. Lord Mountbatten issued an order of the day congratulating all forces involved. Slim in his book *Defeat into Victory* hailed it as 'the turning point of the Burma campaign'. He says 'For the first time a British force had met, held and decisively defeated a major Japanese attack and followed this up by driving the Japanese out of the strongest possible natural positions

British troops consolidate after the capture of Hill 1301, Ngakydauk Pass, Arakan

that they had been preparing for months and were determined to hold at all costs.' (This refers to the final capture of the Maungdaw – Tunnels – Buthidaung line on the 19th/21st March by 5th, 7th, 25th, 26th Divisions assisted by 44th Royal Marine Commando.) 'British and Indian soldiers had proved themselves, man for man, the masters of the best the Japanese could bring against them.' 'It was a victory about which there could be no argument and its effect, not only on the troops engaged but on the whole Fourteenth Army was immense.'

The last sentence was undoubtedly true but the previous one, written in

Lieutenant-General Masakazu Kawabe, commander of Burma Area Army 1943-1944

RAF Regiment man light anti-aircraft position on a beach in Arakan

Australia twelve years after the event, still reads like the necessary propaganda issued at that time in order to boost morale in India and in the rest of the Fourteenth Army. In actual fact, as all men in the Arakan knew, the Japanese were outnumbered by at least ten to one, and the British had overwhelming superiority in armour, heavy artillery and air support.

From the Japanese point of view as Major General Evans states in his biography of Slim, 'despite the fact that Hanaya had failed to destroy 5th and 7th Divisions, Operation "Ha-Go" had succeeded in one important respect – General Slim had been compelled to use his reserves in Arakan as General Kawabe had hoped. It was a bold and courageous venture, for 8,000 Japanese had held XV Corps at bay for close upon three weeks, although at great cost. The gaining and maintenance of air supremacy over the battlefield by Allied Air Forces, the air supply of 7th Division, the fortunate presence of tanks on the east of the Mayu Range, the new fighting spirit of the British and Indian soldiers, and the Japanese inability to resupply all their scattered units, had all contributed to their defeat.'

Slim was still nursing his divisions and had been glad to obtain an opportunity for at least five of them to be 'blooded' and to gain confidence by feeling victorious.

Imphal-Kohima

It will be remembered that from the Japanese point of view, the 'Ha-Go' offensive in the Arakan was but a decoy attack to draw off Slim's reserve divisions before launching a three-division attack (Operation 'U-Go') against IV Corps in the Imphal area. Slim anticipated this strategy and was anxious to obtain the release of his reserves from Christison as soon as possible.

But Slim had underestimated the Japanese potential. He considered that, because of the difficult country and lack of communications, the Japanese would be able to launch and maintain only three regiments at one time between Kohima and the Tiddim area, with some further regiments in reserve.

IV Corps, consisting of 17th, 20th and 23rd Divisions, was spread out over a wide area with road communications to the railhead at Dimapur running for 200 miles parallel to the Japanese front over mountain ranges reaching a height of up to 7,000 feet. A vast engineering effort was being spent on improving this road and building new airfields, hospitals and depots in the flat Imphal plain. But little was done to improve the track running due west from Imphal to Silchar in the Assam Valley, which would have been a much shorter, easier and less vulnerable line of communications. Perhaps GHQ had, in the past, feared a direct route to the plains of Bengal which might allow an invader to penetrate the hill barrier.

Lieutenant-General Scoones had been commanding IV Corps since July 1942. 17th Division had taken part in small patrol actions against the Japanese over the past eighteen months. Under Scoones's guidance they had developed a meticulous and cautious attitude to the Japanese and had built up, perhaps, too much respect for them.

Scoones and Slim had grown up together in the 6th Gurkhas, and academically Scoones was the better general. He wrote carefully thought-out appreciations which usually proved correct, and so Slim learned to respect his judgement. They worked in close harmony, with Scoones providing much of the brainwork, and Slim providing the drive and determination.

The IV Corps infantry consisted of six British, twelve Indian and eleven Gurkha battalions plus some Burmese and Assam battalions attached to Corps HQ. But these infantry were supported in the open Imphal plain by a good tank brigade and a medium regiment of artillery which, if correctly deployed could outgun anything the Japanese could bring forward. Unfortunately, in the battle to come it had underestimated its ammunition requirements and was always short. Due to the nature of the country there was a large engineer contingent both with the corps and working on the roads and airfields. The inhabitants of the area east of the Chindwin, the naked Nagas and the Chins, were not only friendly but fiercely anti-Japanese, and were organised into a most useful series of levies who provided good information.

In the second half of February 1944 a parachute brigade, to be used as infantry, was moved to Kohima.

So all in all by the time of the Japanese offensive Slim had three infantry divisions and a parachute brigade in the Kohima-Imphal-Tiddim area supported by a tank brigade and plenty of artillery. A liability when the fighting started was the vast number of engineer troops and also camp followers in

Above: General Slim with a Gurkha officer examines a captured Japanese sword
Below: Supply column on 17th Division's line of communication in the Chin Hills

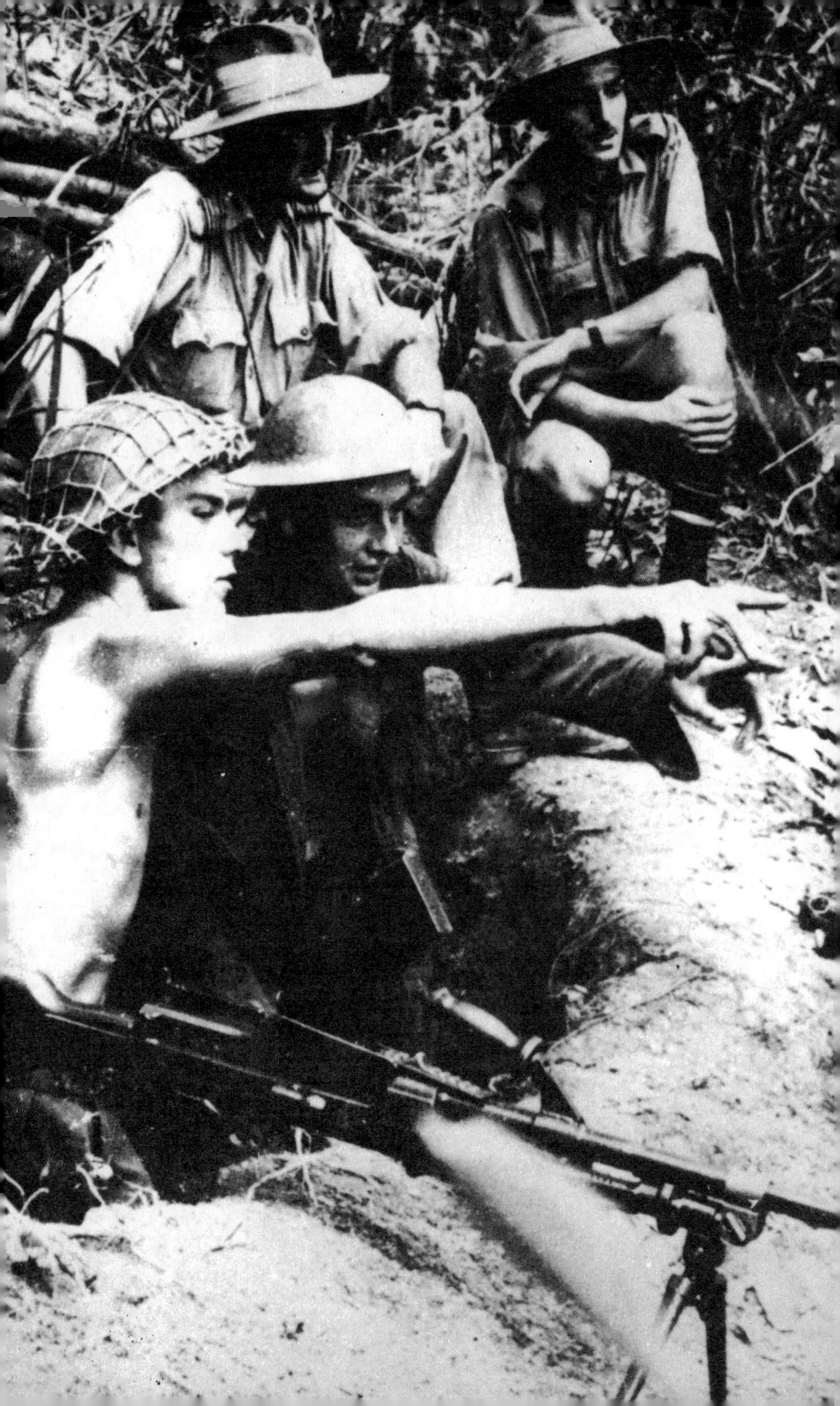

the Imphal plain. Besides corps HQ there were the huge supply, ammunition and petrol dumps, hospitals, workshops and other army and air force installations. The Japanese hoped to replenish their supplies from these dumps.

The RAF had six airstrips on the plain, two of which were all-weather. In the fortress area around corps and RAF HQ there were 51,000 men of all ranks. Many of these were to be later evacuated by air as being useless mouths to feed.

Slim had three courses open to him when considering the defence. He could, as in the Arakan, order all three divisions to hold their extended positions while being supplied by air, and then launch a counterattack from Dimapur with his army reserves. But these divisions, brigades and battalions had not practiced the receipt of air supply, which would be difficult but not impossible in the hills, and they did not yet have full confidence in it. Leaving the divisions where they were would mean that the supply and maintenance organization in the Imphal plain would be highly vulnerable, and it was essential that supplies did not fall into Japanese hands. Also the troops would feel more isolated in their extended positions and would be more likely to give way.

Slim's second option was to attempt a counterattack before the Japanese offensive was launched. With his troops disposed as they were, untrained for attack and with morale, after two years in the malarial hills, not being particularly high, this choice was not on. It was better for such troops to resist in defence and wear down the enemy who would be a long way from base, until such time as they were comparatively strong enough to attack. Anyway the fly-in of the Chindits overhead into central Burma was a form of army counter-

RAF Regiment defends a forward air field on the Imphal Plain

Air Marshal Sir John Baldwin, commander of Third Tactical Air Force

attack against the Japanese communications.

The third possibility, which Slim chose, was to concentrate on the Imphal plain where there were airfields, supplies, reserves of ammunition and above all tanks, and defend it as a fortress until such time as the Japanese were worn down, and a counterattack from Assam could come to the rescue. It was essential that reinforcements should be flown in as soon as they were released from the Arakan where the Ha-Go offensive had tied them down. The danger was that the divisions would be unable to disengage themselves in time to retreat to the Imphal plain in good order and then be able to fight as formed units. Also once a retreat starts it affects the whole mentality of an army and it is difficult to stop. It was here that Slim had to show all his determination, outward calmness and self confidence, courage and steadfastness. The tactical battle would initially have to be fought by Scoones and the RAF, while Slim stood in the wings arranging for relief.

The role of the RAF was to be crucial. Third Tactical Air Force (TAF) had been formed on 18th December 1943, with Air Marshal Baldwin in command, and was responsible for all supply dropping activities in the Fourteenth Army area during the Imphal battle. Baldwin's own military experience in both the army and the airforce suited him well for close cooperation with the army, and after the re-shuffle in which South East Asia Command was set up he worked in close conjunction with Slim. For two years they lived in the same officers' mess, and he helped Slim a great deal with air matters of which Slim had had little previous experience.

In December 1943 he had twenty-three squadrons of fighters and fighter bombers under his command, and this was increased as the fighting at Imphal stepped up in March 1944.

As an illustration of the relative intensity of the air effort which played such a vital part in the defence of Imphal and the subsequent defeat of the Japanese, the latter flew only 1,750 sorties between 10th March and 30th July. During the same period the RAF fighter squadrons of Third TAF flew 18,660 sorties, and the USAAF fighter squadrons 10,800 sorties. Their losses were 130 RAF and 40 USAAF aircraft destroyed or missing.

In addition to its operations at Imphal, Third TAF was also responsible for supplying the Chindit forces. The first of these flew in to Burma on the night of 5th-6th March, just as the Japanese with three divisions were preparing to cross the Chindwin in the opposite direction to attack IV Corps in the Imphal-Tiddim area. Slim was officially responsible for these forces, and also for the three Chinese divisions under Stilwell which were slowly advancing south from North-East Assam, along the Ledo road. In practice, he was not so closely concerned with them as with the troops on the Imphal and Arakan fronts, and he had mixed feelings about the whole Chindit enterprise. We shall examine their role, and Slim's place in it, later. Meanwhile, the Chindits' presence behind the Japanese front throughout the Imphal fighting should not be forgotten.

So the Japanese had three divisions plus the doubtful addition of the Indian National Army (about a brigade strength), to attack three British-Indian divisions, one tank brigade, one parachute brigade and a preponderance of artillery. The British also had air dominance over the area and were surrounded by friendly tribesmen in the hills from whose organised levies good information could be obtained.

Slim had estimated that the Japanese, due to administrative difficulties, could commit only three regiments to such an offensive. However, when reports came through early in March that 33rd Division had arrived in the Kabaw valley complete with a regiment of light tanks and two regiments of heavy artillery, General Scoones knew that he must revise his plan of defence.

IV Corps were spread over 175 miles from Kohima in the north to Fort White in the south, and from Imphal in the centre to Sittaung 75 miles to the east on the Chindwin River.

The two brigades of 17th Division were among the hills in the Tongzang-Tiddim area supported by two brigades of 23rd Division to their rear. The remaining brigade of 23rd Division was held as reserve in the Imphal plain. 17th Division had during its two years of occupation built up an administrative area including a hospital at Milestone 109 which, in spite of the experience in the Arakan, was undefended.

20th Division was based on Tamu with forward positions at Sittaung and down the Yu River.

In the Imphal plain Scoones had 23rd Division's 37th Brigade and the

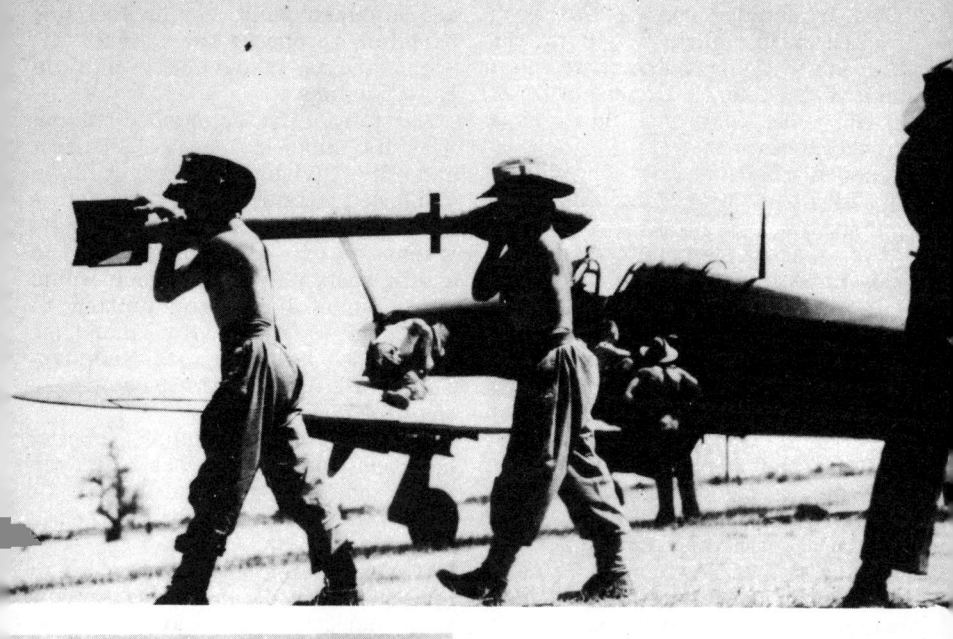

Armourers load a rocket onto a Hurricane at an Imphal airstrip

Japanese soldiers at Army HQ in the Burma summer capitol of Maymyo

Lieutenant-General Renya Mutaguchi, the 'Conqueror of Singapore' and Commander Fifteenth Army in Burma

254th Tank Brigade in reserve.

The parachute brigade had been directed on to Ukhrul to protect the approach to Kohima, and there was a small detachment in the hills at Jessami, due east of Ukhrul, as a further protection.

These dispositions were very vulnerable to attack by a determined and confident enemy.

The Japanese plan of attack divided their force into three. In the south, the Japanese 33rd Division was to surround Cowan's 17th Division, cutting off its communications with Imphal, while a column under Major General Yamomoto moved north up the Kalemyo-Tamu road and then west to Palel and Imphal. This column, advancing along roads, had most of the tanks and heavy artillery.

In the centre, 15th Division, after crossing the Chindwin, was to move south of Ukhrul along jungle tracks against the Imphal road immediately to the north of the Imphal Plain. 31st Division was to cross the Chindwin between Tamanthi and Homalin and advance over a formidable mountain range to capture Kohima.

The southern offensive by 33rd Division was intended to start a week before the two divisions on their right, in order to draw Allied reserves away from Imphal and Kohima. Mutaguchi hoped that 33rd Division, with its tanks and armour would open a road communication between his forward positions at Kalewa and Kalemyo to the Imphal plain within three or four weeks when the supplies carried by the two northern divisions were due to run out. He also hoped to replenish his food and petrol supplies from the dumps in the 17th Division and Imphal areas. He did not intend to spend much time on eliminating 17th Division but to press on north leaving behind a small containing force, including an INA battalion to beseige them in the Tiddim-Fort White areas if necessary.

15th Division was not up to strength when the offensive started and consisted of only six infantry battalions and eighteen guns, having lost one battalion to oppose the Chindit airborne landing. It was also to move in three columns.

Apart from the Yamamoto column with its tanks and heavy artillery, and 33rd Division's reserve column and headquarters, all the other forces would have to travel along jungle tracks across high mountains to attain their objectives. They would carry supplies and ammunition to last them three weeks, by which time they hoped that the road Kalemyo-Tamu-Palel-Imphal would be open to them for wheeled traffic.

For this enterprise dumps of supplies had been made along the Chindwin River and along tracks leading to the Chindwin from the railways in central Burma.

It was an ambitious plan, a hit or miss plan, for if they failed to take their objectives the Japanese were lost. But the Japanese at that time, and Mutaguchi 'the victor of Singapore' in particular, held the British – Indian divisions in such scorn that no question of failure entered their heads. In Burma Area Army HQ there was was not nearly so much confidence especially among the Japanese 5th Air Division who openly predicted failure.

For long hours, Scoones conferred with Slim on the problems facing him. It was decided to fight and win the battle on the Imphal plain around their own dumps of supplies. For this to be successful all unwanted mouths including thousands of indentured labourers working on the roads and airfields, would have to be evacuated.

17th and 20th Divisions would fall back into the plain. It was intended that 17th Division would make a clean break when ordered. It would leave one brigade on the Tiddim road at the entrance of the plain and the headquarters and the other brigade would come into corps reserve. Main features of the road would be demolished as they retired.

JAPANESE THRUST ON IMPHAL - KOHIMA

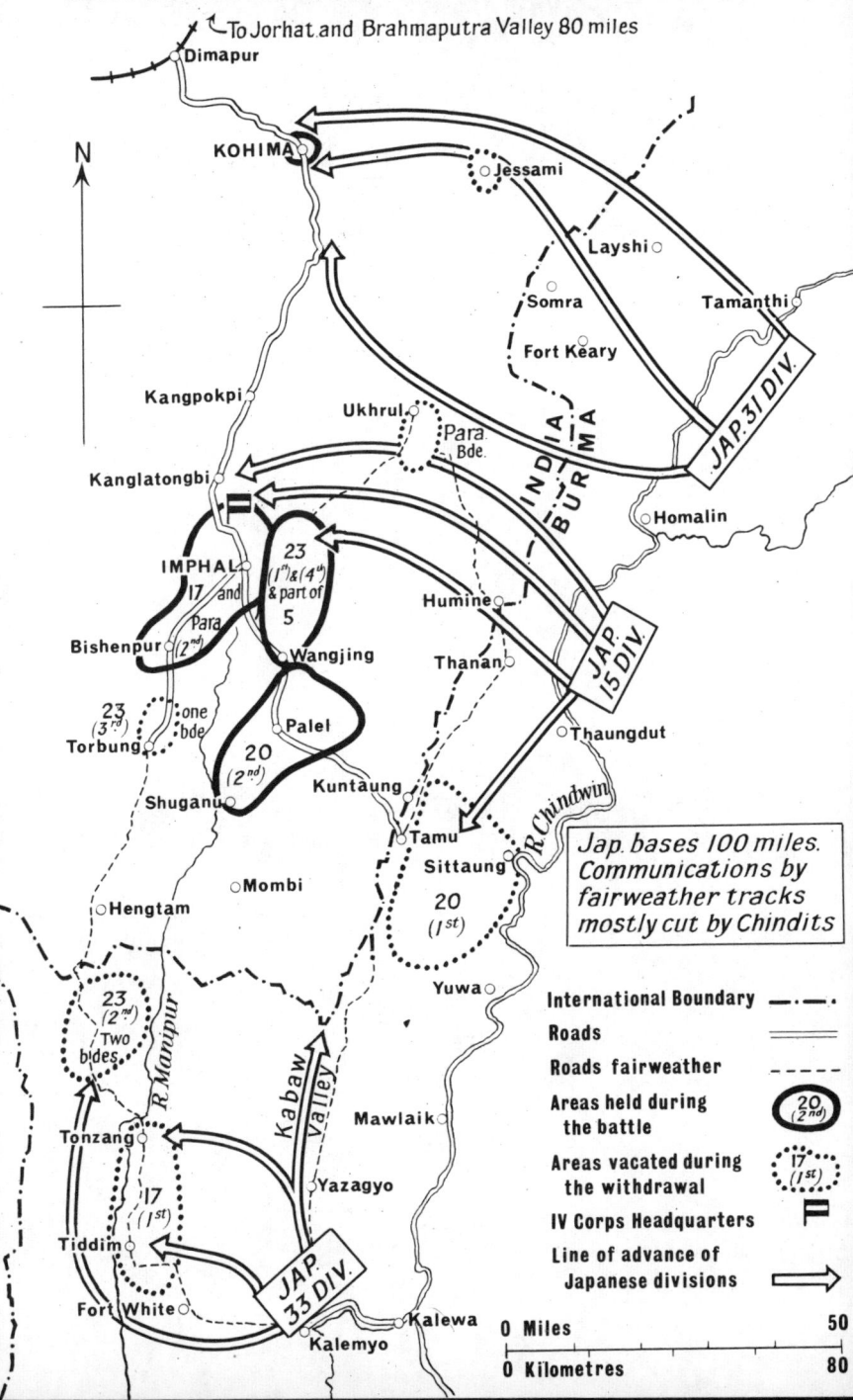

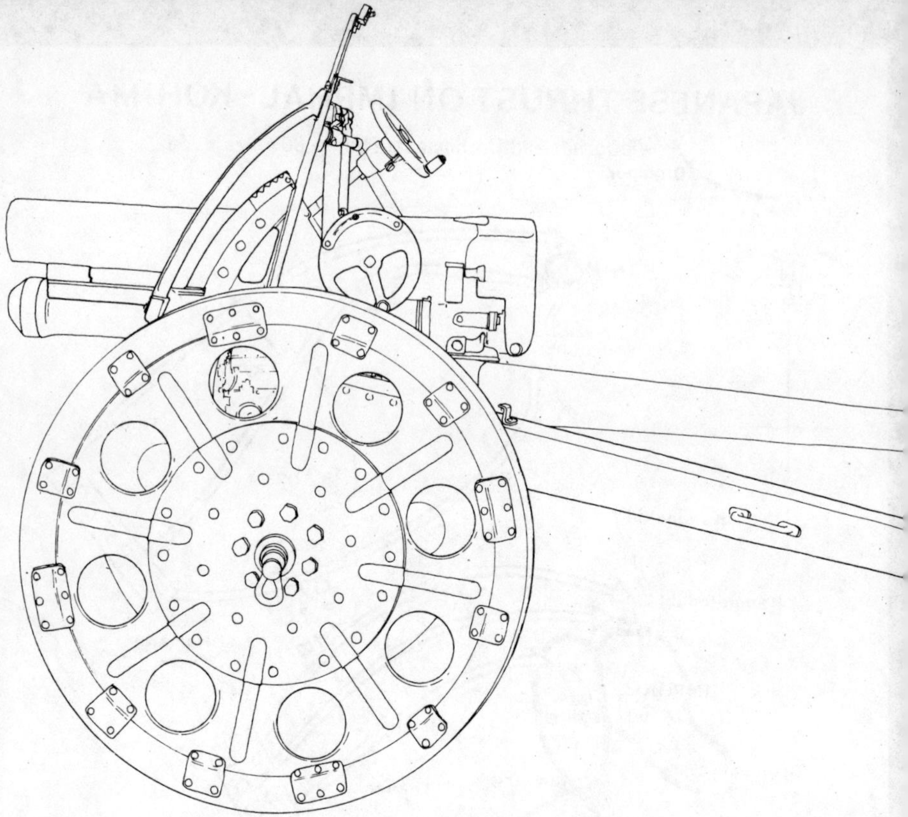

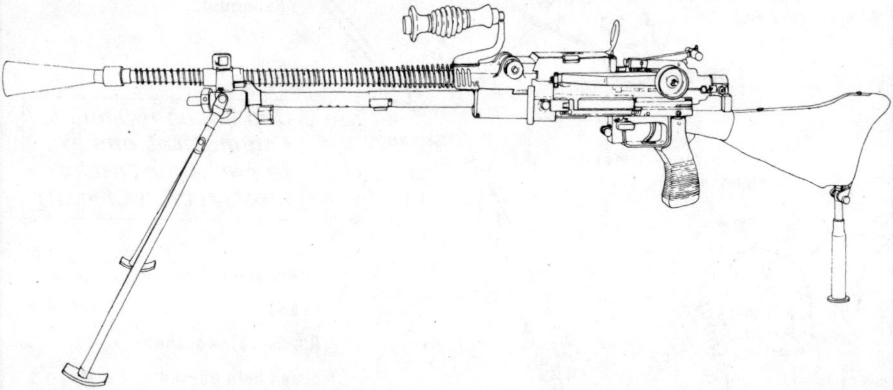

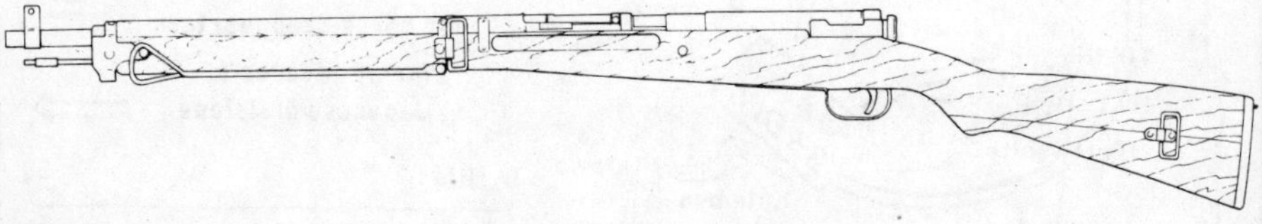

The Japanese 70mm Model 92 (1932) howitzer. This is the Japanese army's standard infantry support howitzer and, with its small size and provision for being drawn by horses, was very handy for use in such countries as Burma. *Weight:* 486lbs. *Weight of shell:* 8.36lbs. *Range:* 1,500 yards effective, 3,000 yards maximum. *Rate of fire:* Ten rounds per minute

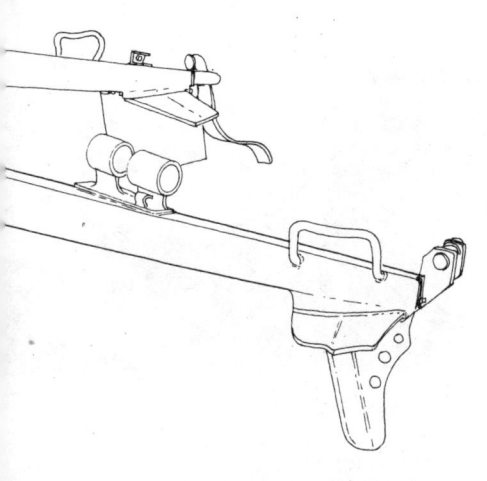

The Japanese 7.7mm Model 99 (1939) light machine gun. This was the Japanese army's companion for the Model 99 rifle, when it was realised that lightweight infantry weapons, with consequent excellent mobility, must give way to heavier weapons with better firepower. Its nearest equivalent in the Allied armies was the British Bren gun. *Calibre:* 7.7mm. *Operation:* Gas, automatic. *Overall length:* 46.75 inches. *Barrel length:* 21.5 inches. *Feed:* Detachable box magazine holding 30 rounds. *Weight:* 23lbs. *Muzzle velocity:* 2,350 feet per second. *Cyclic rate of fire:* 850 rounds per minute

The Japanese 7.7mm Model 99 (1939) rifle. This was introduced to supplant the earlier 6.5mm rifle, which had been found during combat experience in China to be too small a calibre weapon for modern war. It was basically a scaled up version of the Model 38 (1905) it was designed to replace, which was in turn an adaptation of the German Mauser Gewehr 98. A feature common to both the Model 38 and Model 99 rifles was the provision of a sliding cover over the breech to keep dirt out when the bolt was being worked, but Japanese troops often removed it as it made a considerable amount of noise. Another notable feature was the monopod under the fore part of the barrel, to steady the rifle when it was being fired on the ground. *Calibre:* 7.7mm. *Operation:* Turn bolt. *Overall length:* 50 inches. *Barrel length:* 31.4 inches. *Feed:* Non-detachable box magazine holding five rounds. *Weight:* 9.1lbs. *Muzzle velocity:* 2,390 feet per second

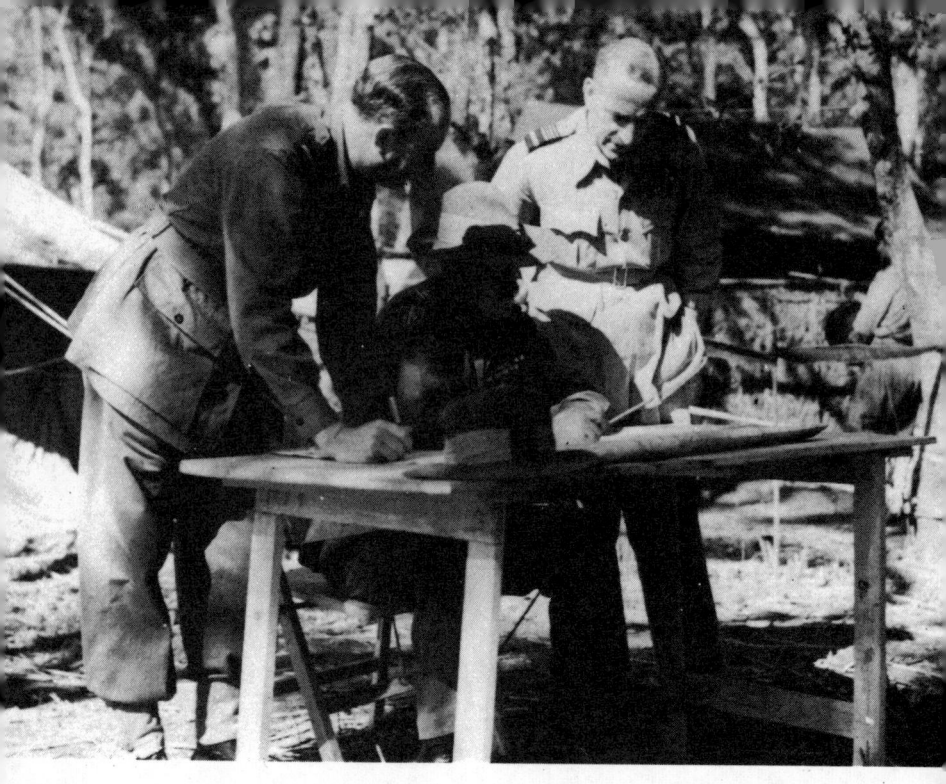

Air Vice-Marshal S F Vincent (left) and Air Marshal Coryton (right) with General Slim at Fourteenth Army HQ

20th Division, which was facing east with its communications protected behind it and at right angles to the front, would maintain its position in front of Tamu, but be prepared to retire when ordered. One of its objects would be to evacuate or destroy its administrative dumps at Moreh, always a task that damaged morale.

23rd Division would also come into Corps reserve with special responsibility for keeping the road open to Kohima. IV Corps would thus have, if all went well, one and a half infantry divisions and the armoured brigade as a mobile reserve.

Slim also decided to reinforce his central front by flying in a division from the Arakan.

In judgement after the event there is no doubt that this was a good plan. The difficulty would be for the forward divisions to disengage and retire in trucks along a 100-mile thin tenuous road link through jungle covered hills and parallel to the front. But 17th Division, whose first taste of battle was in South Burma in 1942, was the most experienced division of all at this sort of operation although they were now once again handicapped with too much motor transport and supplies dumped for offensive action.

Having watched the start of the fly-in of 77th Brigade into Central Burma on the evening of 5th March Slim went to IV Corps Headquarters at Imphal. Here he again discussed with Scoones plans to meet the expected Japanese offensive. Slim reluctantly agreed to Scoones' plan for the withdrawal of 17th and 20th Divisions but with the proviso that the order to withdraw should be given personally by Scoones to the divisional commander only when he was certain that a major offensive had begun. After all his retreats Slim did not want to retreat again, especially as the Indian Army had been earning a bad reputation over the years in this respect. But this proviso was to result in the withdrawal of 17th Division being left too late.

Scoones organised his defence of the Imphal Plain by initiating a series of defended administrative 'boxes' around the supply dumps and airfields in the Imphal Plain. He had been wise enough, learning from the experience in the Arakan, to teach all engineers, corps artillery, reserve infantry battalions and RAF regiments how to defend themselves, and he had appointed commanders with a small staff for each box. Later these boxes were withdrawn within a central perimeter circling the vital airfields and some stores had to be abandoned. Engineer labour was transferred from road construction to prepare defensive positions.

Cowan's 17th Division was still under an old order to attack Kalemyo. But he had been told of the possibility of his withdrawal to Imphal without being able to rely on corps reserve assistance.

Gracey of 20th Division, while still patrolling offensively, had wisely issued his plan for withdrawal to all his brigadiers and senior staff officers. He himself only was to give the final order to withdraw.

On 9th March a two-man Gurkha patrol reported the crossing of the Manipur river by 2,000 Japanese accompanied by guns and mules just south of the Tiddim-Fort White defended area, but the report was not confirmed, and was disbelieved. Tongzang in 17th Division's rear was attacked from the east on 10th March. Cowan reacted only slightly. It should be remembered that the division had been in the area for eighteen months and many hair-raising reports had been found to be false.

Japanese artillery penetrate the Imphal Plain

Behind Gracey's 20th Division the Japanese had also infiltrated in large numbers, but their first attack in the Kabaw Valley south of Tamu was successfully repulsed on 11th March.

By now Scoones was convinced that the Japanese offensive had begun. On the 13th he gave Cowan permission to withdraw 17th Division to the Imphal plain, and told Gracey to evacuate all engineer and labour units, prior to withdrawing 20th Division.

Gracey's well thought out plan of withdrawal was put into effect and, with one or two hitches, worked remarkably well. By the 21st his division was all across the Yu river, and in the following days he withdrew to the heights of Shenam, without any unit being cut off.

Cowan was slow to issue orders for the retreat, and held on for another vital twenty-four hours before ordering it to start at 0500 hours the next day. He also ordered all surplus supplies to be destroyed. As he had not warned any of his commanders that such a withdrawal might take place, these orders came as a complete surprise. By now there were four Japanese road blocks on the division's long and difficult line of retreat, with detachments and supply dumps isolated between them. Cowan's rear brigade held the vital Manipur river bridge, so that 17th Division could cross the river, but Scoones was obliged to commit his reserves from the Imphal plain in order to extricate it.

Reinforcements were clearly needed. Giffard had instructed Slim to disengage some of his divisions in the Arakan, while Mountbatten was obtaining the agreement of both British and American Chiefs of Staff and of the elusive Stilwell to take American aircraft off the 'Hump' route to China, in order to move the 5th Division from Arakan to Imphal. By 20th March the first brigade of 5th Division had been airlanded in the Imphal plain. Scoones quickly sent one battalion to Kohima, keeping the remainder in reserve.

General Stopford, commander of XXXIII Corps during the Imphal battle

XXXIII Corps under Lieutenant-General Stopford was the War Office theatre reserve, and after many comings and goings among senior Allied officers, it was finally decided that this, with the British 2nd Division, would come under Slim's command to relieve the pressure on Imphal. 23rd LRP (Chindit) Brigade would come under XXXIII Corps, and 14th LRP Brigade would be held in readiness to assist. Wingate complained bitterly at this diversion of his forces from the offensive penetration operations for which they were designed, and in the end 14th Brigade was returned to him.

Slim's real anxiety was the long and precarious line of communication to Kohima and beyond to railhead at Dimapur, where there were 45,000 administrative troops of whom only 500 knew how to fire a rifle. If the Japanese debouched into the Brahmaputra valley they would not only cut off IV Corps, but also Stilwell on the Ledo front and the huge airforce and hospital complex in north eastern Assam. At this juncture Stilwell offered to stop his offensive and to despatch a Chinese division to help the British out of their predicament. With the reinforcements he had obtained, Slim instead ordered Stopford's XXXIII Corps to concentrate at the Dimapur railhead and to hold and keep the road clear as far as Kohima. These orders took effect on 27th March as the situation worsened on all fronts. The forward elements of British 2nd Division and 23rd LRP Brigade could not arrive before 2nd April, but by 29th March Sato's 31st Division had already cut the road between Imphal and Kohima.

Now the four divisions and three brigades of IV Corps were isolated by road from the rest of the army. 17th Division, however, had compensated for their slow start by the skill and audacity with which they cleared the road blocks on their line of retreat. On the way, they inflicted so many casualties that the Japanese divisional commander, Yanagida, recommended to Mutaguchi that the offensive should stop. Mutaguchi was so annoyed that he fired Yanagida on the spot. By 4th April, 17th Division managed to withdraw nearly all their men, mules, weapons and trucks to the Imphal plain, having carried out extensive demolition in their rear which seriously impeded the advance of Japanese tanks and medium artillery. 5th Division was flying in, giving Scoones a total strength equivalent to five divisions (17th, 20th, 23rd, 5th, Parachute Brigade and tank brigade), against the three Japanese divisions.

The errors in Slim's plan of defence were firstly that he underestimated the size of the Japanese offensive, and secondly that he should have given Scoones more incisive orders on the withdrawal of his forward divisions. In his book, Slim blames his own judgement for both of these mistakes.

It was natural that the Japanese, with their fanatical offensive spirit and in spite of their almost criminal neglect of the administrative consequences of this thrust into India at a distance of between 100 and 200 miles from their bases, should at first call the tune and impose their will on the British forces.

In a long battle, however, the Japanese were at a disadvantage. Since they had to use mere footpaths over the tops of mountains up to 7,500 feet high, the forces making these thrusts were lightly equipped. Their bases were far away across the Chindwin, they had comparatively little artillery, and they had to trust for their future supplies on Imphal falling and 33rd Division opening up a lorry route from Kalewa.

Whilst Mutaguchi was starting to throttle IV Corps, the Chindits were getting their grip on the Japanese 18th and 56th Divisions opposing Stilwell and the Chinese armies to the east. It now became a question of who could squeeze hardest. With Allied air dominance over the skies of Burma and with transport aircraft made available by Churchill and Roosevelt, the Allied forces could continue to breathe due to air supply until such time as the Japanese had to relinquish their grip.

Mutaguchi allowed his forces three weeks to achieve their objective. He had grossly underestimated both the British-Indian resistance and his own administrative difficulties. He had not even followed the traditional Chinese tactic of leaving your surrounded enemy a loophole for retreat so that he would not resist too much. IV Corps were forced to resist and even the victor of Singapore should have realised that after more than two years of war both British and Indian troops would have become better trained and more experienced and with ever-improving technical capabilities. Mutaguchi was still calling the tune but the determined Slim was letting the Japanese forces lose their momentum and wear themselves out

The Japanese 90mm Model 94 (1934) mortar. A sturdy but somewhat heavy weapon, the Model 94 saw widespread service with Japanese infantry units. Towards the end of the war it was joined by another mortar of the same calibre, the Model 97 (1937), which was considerably lighter as a result of the abandoning of the recoil mechanism and the lightening of other parts. *Weight:* 340lbs. *Length of barrel:*: 51.75 inches. *Range:* 612 to 4,155 yards depending on the type of bomb used

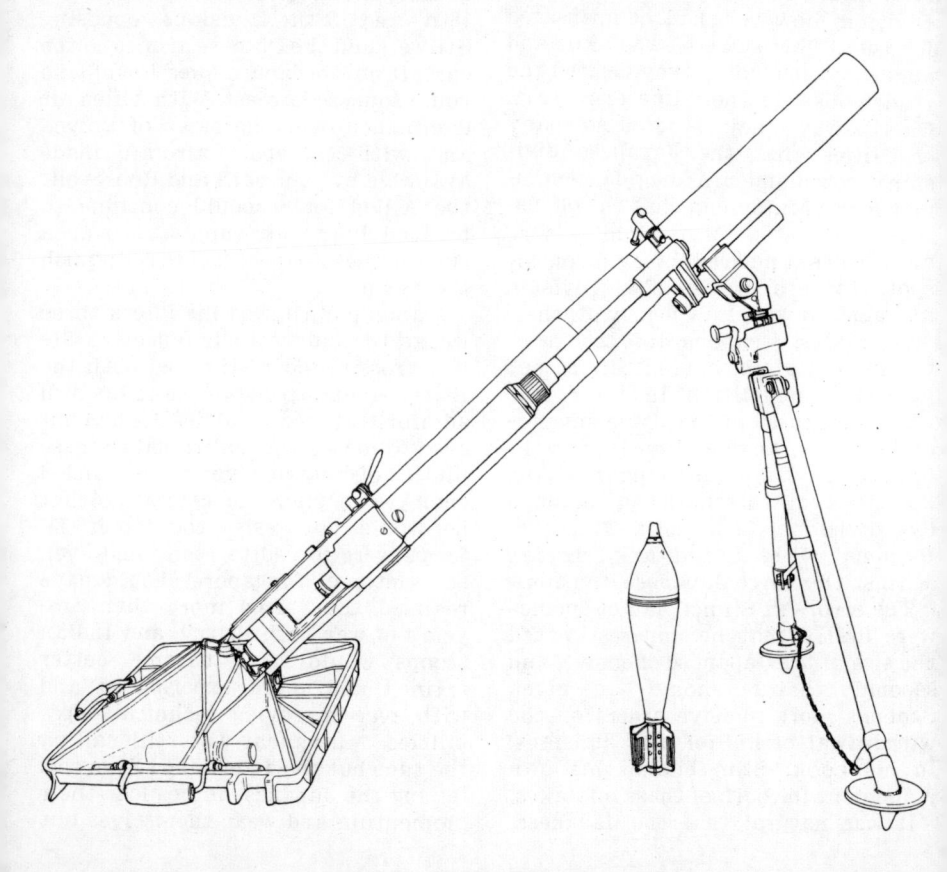

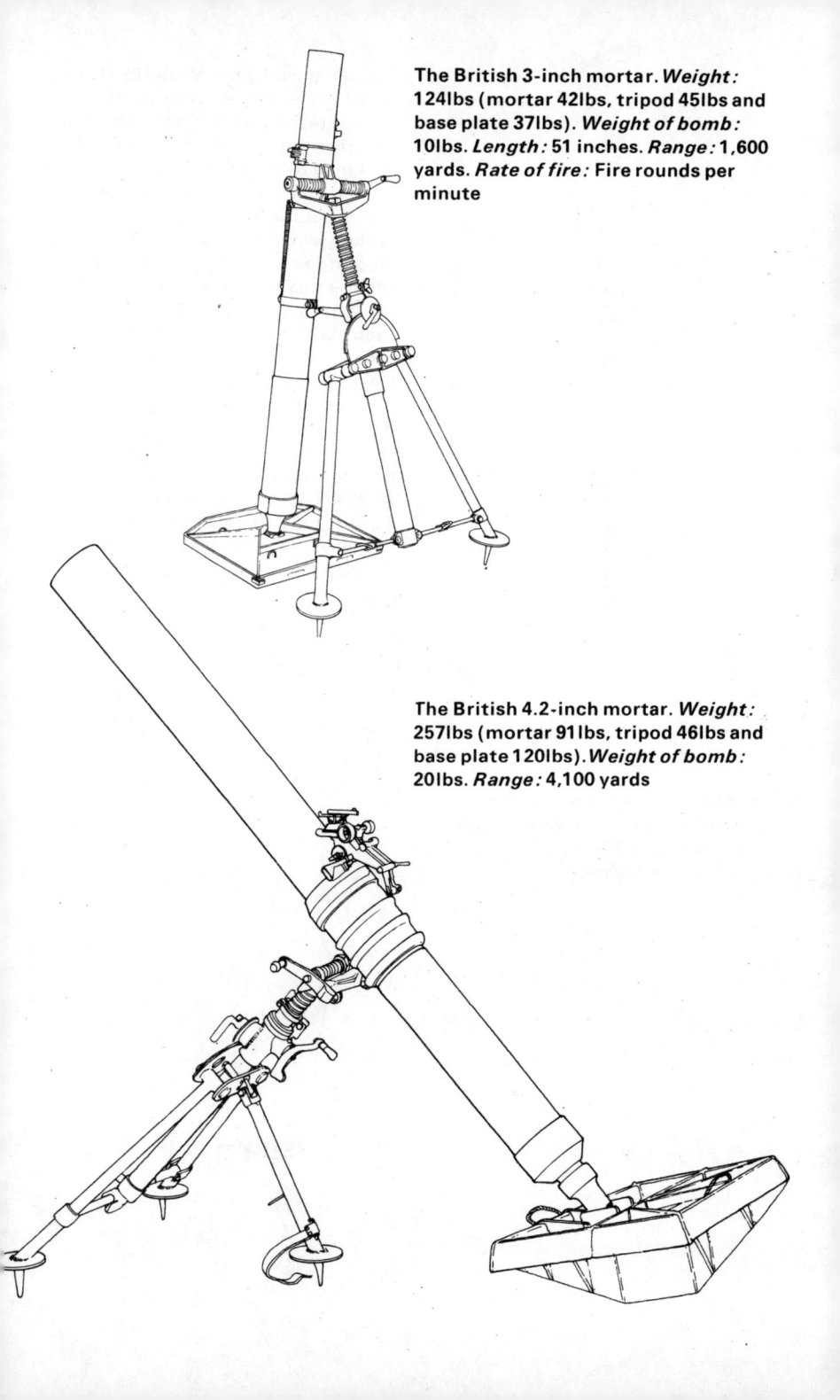

The British 3-inch mortar. *Weight:* 124lbs (mortar 42lbs, tripod 45lbs and base plate 37lbs). *Weight of bomb:* 10lbs. *Length:* 51 inches. *Range:* 1,600 yards. *Rate of fire:* Fire rounds per minute

The British 4.2-inch mortar. *Weight:* 257lbs (mortar 91lbs, tripod 46lbs and base plate 120lbs). *Weight of bomb:* 20lbs. *Range:* 4,100 yards

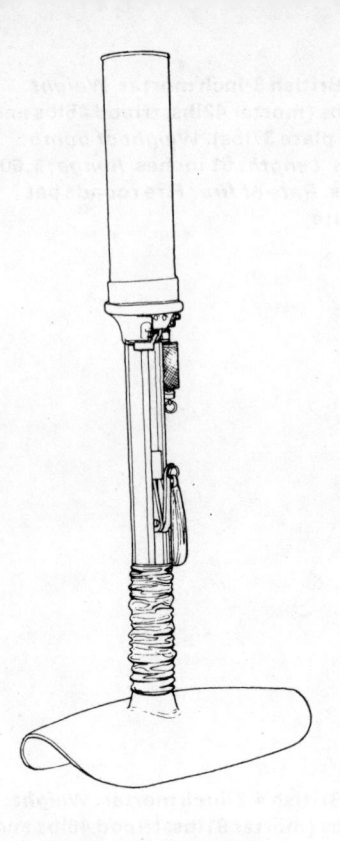

The Japanese 50mm Model 89 (1929) grenade discharger. When first encountered in action, this discharger was thought by Allied troops to be designed to be fired with the base plate resting on the knee and lower thigh. This would in fact cause the leg to be broken when the weapon was discharged. Issue of the dischargers seems to have been on the scale of three or four to the weapons section of each platoon. The range attained by the grenade was dependent on the elevation of the discharger and the position of the trigger housing in the barrel, which increased or decreased the length of barrel travelled by the grenade, and hence its range. *Weight:* 10.25 lbs. *Weight of grenade:* 1lb 12ozs. *Range:* 700 yards maximum. Optimum range was 65-175 yards. *Rate of fire:* 18 to 20 rounds per minute

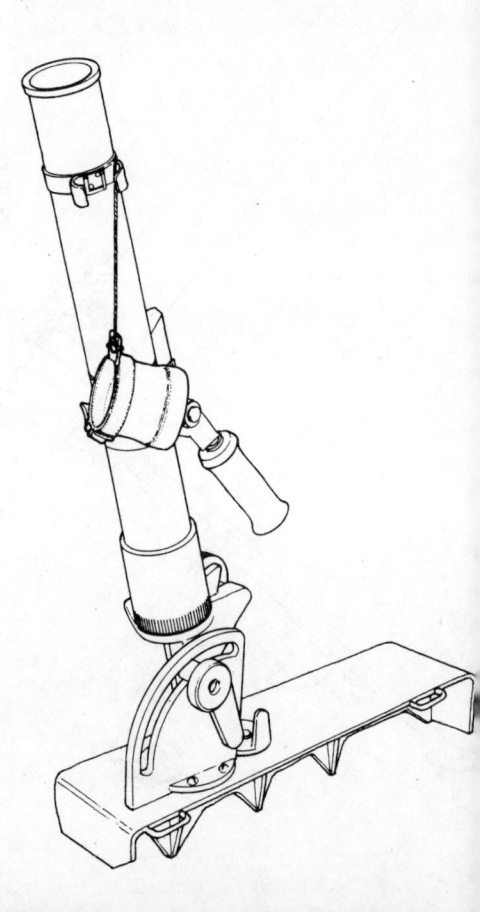

The British 2-inch mortar. *Weight:* 32.5lbs. *Weight of bomb:* 2lbs. *Length.* 25 inches. *Range:* 470 yards. *Rate of fire:* Five rounds per minute

while he gathered and deployed fresh reserves.

At the end of March, it seemed that the whole of the Japanese 31st Division was advancing on Kohima and Dimapur. 161st Brigade of 5th Division was flown into Dimapur. Slim ordered it to Kohima, a vital pass which was the key both to a Japanese advance on Dimapur, and to the relief of Imphal by road. 161st Brigade's commander, Brigadier Warren, immediately set out to contact the enemy.

Meanwhile, Lieutenant-General Stopford had taken command in the area as his XXXIII Corps started to arrive. Stopford's previous experience had been in Europe, and his cautious and deliberate methods were better suited to European warfare than to Assam. He had also to train his staff which was new to the game. Slim at first found him rather slow and stereotyped, but he grew out of this cautious phase as a result of Slim's constant insistence on greater speed.

Acting on the old Staff College adage of 'concentration at the vital point', Stopford ordered 161st Brigade back to Dimapur, despite Warren's protests, only to have to return it to Kohima when the Japanese attacked a few days later. In fact, 31st Division's orders were to take Kohima, and not advance on Dimapur until the road from the south was open, though of course Slim and Stopford were not to know this. Had Warren remained in the Kohima area, the battle there would probably have been won earlier, and the road to Imphal more quickly opened. In the event Kohima was held by the supreme heroism of its small garrison for nearly two months, before Stopford could advance to its relief.

Stopford deployed his 2nd Division in the Brahmaputra valley to protect communications there against possible attack. Slim, however, was rather impatient of Stopford's deliberate methods, and on 8th April relieved him of this task, moving 3rd Commando Brigade from the Arakan coast to take it over. Slim did not like commandoes any more than he liked airborne forces so the highly trained British Commandoes were given this ignoble role. Soon afterwards, a Chindit column captured a set of 31st Division's operation orders, which showed that the valley was not threatened.

On 10th April, with Giffard's agreement, Slim ordered a general offensive. Scoones' IV Corps was to hold the Japanese 33rd Division south of Imphal and, using interior lines, to attack 15th and 33rd Divisions in turn. They were also to direct a force onto Ukhrul to cut the communications of 31st Division.

Stopford, whose leading brigade had made contact with Warren's brigade overlooking Kohima, was to hold Kohima as a starting point to destroy 31st Division. This he would do by establishing a force on the Jessami – Kharasom area behind 31st Division, and then striking with his main force down the Imphal Road.

Stilwell was to press on with his advance down the Ledo Road, and not to worry about his rear. The Chindits (Special Force) would step up operations in order to aid Stilwell's advance and draw away reserves.

There were sufficient aircraft available for both Stilwell's forces and the Chindits to remain on air supply as well as to maintain two brigades of XXXIII Corps and one of IV Corps. IV Corps would rely on its dumps and air-landed supplies. The transport aircraft would continue to evacuate all unnecessary mouths from the Imphal Plain.

This order set the scene of operation for the next two months.

As soon as XXXIII Corps had started to get into position, and as soon as Slim had located all the Japanese regiments of the three divisions opposing him, he had immediately ordered an offensive. A good method of offense is to engage all known enemy and keep them engaged so that they have no time for any other

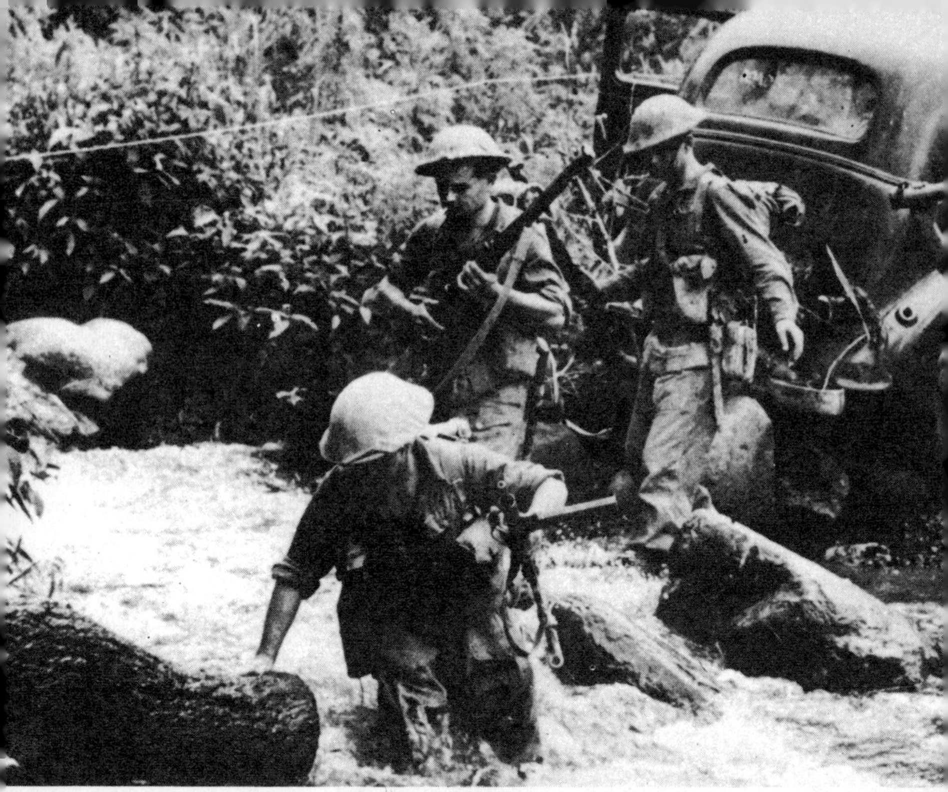

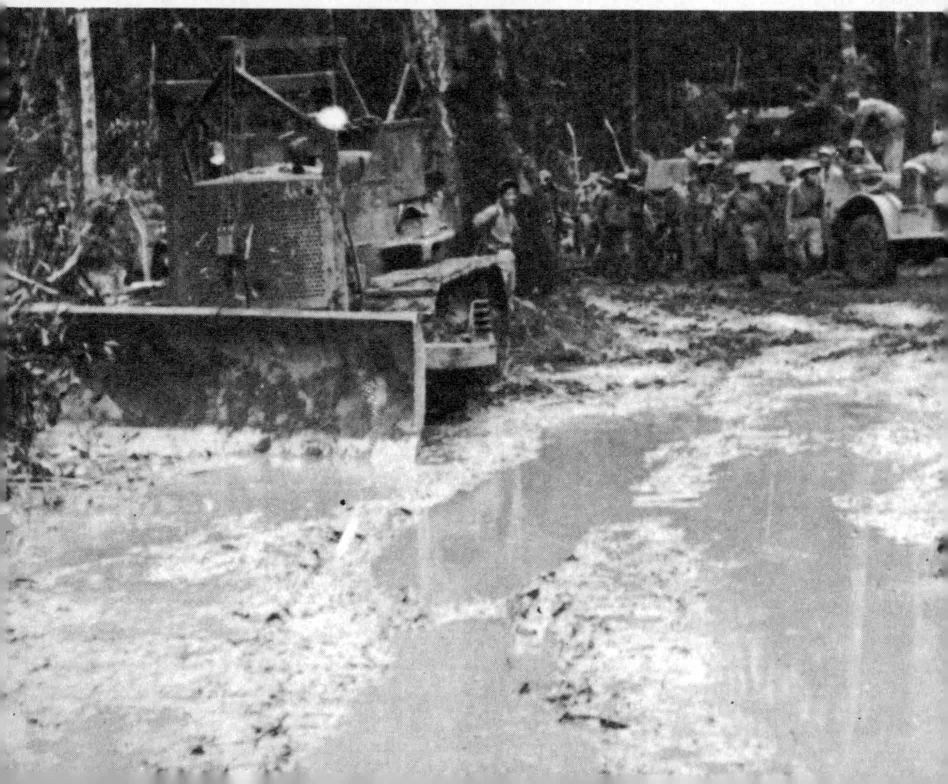

Corporal Edwards of North Wales leads his section on the Imphal-Kohima front

manoeuvre. Slim had started to impose his will on the enemy at the earliest possible moment. He had been the one never to doubt that the Japanese, if British supply bases were held, would lose their momentum and initiative. It shows Slim's resilience after two and a half years of unsuccessful campaigning for him to seize the initiative at this early date. The decision was his alone and he still had to be the driving force behind his two corps, Stilwell and a slightly hesitant Special Force suffering from the death of its leader. 2nd British Division had had no previous experience of jungle warfare and had not been specifically trained for it. Some of IV Corps' generals could not be criticised if they appeared a little weary and cautious when faced once more with this formidable, savage and

Chinese troops advance down Hukawng Valley towards Kamaing and Mogaung

tearaway enemy. But Slim, from now on, did not leave them in peace and exhorted and urged them on to throw caution aside and attack the enemy wherever he could be found.

The total force Slim had deployed against Mutaguchi's three divisions, now running short of supplies, was the equivalent of almost nine divisions, but it was still difficult, despite air supply, to bring them all to bear.

On the Imphal Plain the Japanese were trying to apply pressure on all sides. 33rd Division was attacking 17th Division which was now covering the Imphal - Silchar track leading directly west to the plain of Bengal. 20th Division was still on the heights of Shenam between Tamu and the Imphal plain and was valiantly resisting Yamamoto's 213th Infantry Regiment supported by his tank regiment and medium artillery brought up from Kalemyo. Scoones had been ordered to take Ukhrul and he had launched his 5th and 23rd Divisions to do so, but they were making heavy weather of it along this single track up into the high hills against the resistance of the Japanese 15th Division.

Scoones's main trouble was supply. Ration scales had been reduced, Scoones asked for supply aircraft to operate by night as well as by day and Air Marshal Baldwin, now in charge of this operation, did his best to comply within his limited resources. Scoones still had the equivalent of over five divisions to oppose the two attacking him, and had overwhelming

British anti-tank gunners blast a Japanese bunker in the Tiddim Hills

be enough roads to carry all the vehicles which they think that formation might possibly need. They forget that marching on foot with a few trucks for supplies is a remarkably swift way of carrying out an advance, as the Japanese had again and again proved, and that after a certain optimum, trucks became more of a hindrance than a help.

However the Allies could not hope to match the Japanese fanatical courage and willingness to die. As John Masters has said in his *The Road past Mandalay*, nearly every Japanese soldier could have been awarded a Victoria Cross or Congressional Medal of Honour if judged by British and American standards. Consequently the Allies had to bring to bear the maximum amount of their technical superiority to offset this *kamikaze* spirit. Massive close air support strikes and prolonged heavy artillery and mortar bombardment were the order of the day. Tanks had to be winched into position so that their guns could knock out a Japanese bunker position which might hold up the advance of 500 infantry. Bulldozers were used in conjunction with tanks and medium artillery so that they could be moved into positions where they could bring their guns to bear in this most difficult jungle-covered mountainous country.

Slim did not alter the aim he had had from the beginning – to take advantage of the Japanese capacity for attack by letting it destroy them. The Japanese were 100 miles or more from their bases. The Chindits had cut two out of three of their lines of communication. As long as the Japanese attacked they would use up ammunition and petrol and have no time to collect food. So they would wear themselves out like flies hurling themselves against a window while Slim prepared his fly killer.

air superiority, so there was no chance that his troops would now fold.

Slim was being exhorted to 'relieve' Imphal but he thought that it was more important to defeat the enemy. So he urged his two corps to carry out the encircling movements via Jessami and Ukhrul. The Japanese would be free to withdraw at the onset of the monsoon and he wanted them to retire defeated, not in their own time.

Kohima had now been contacted and there was no question of its fall. Stopford's 2nd Division was learning the art of jungle warfare and finding that it had too many trucks and other unnecessary appendages for this type of warfare. When preparing a war establishment, staff officers rarely take into account whether there will

Lieutenant-General Kotuku Sato, commander of the 31st Division which attacked Kohima in March-April 1944

Stopford ordered Perowne's 23rd Long Range Penetration brigade to advance onto Ukhrul to encircle and outflank the Japanese. Stopford was now making the running while Scoones held on, his 5th and 23rd Divisions having made little headway towards Ukhrul.

Scoone's IV Corps came in for some criticism from the General Staff in London at their apparent lethargy. This was shown by Lord Mountbatten's signal to Giffard asking him 'when can you start your offensive north' (from the Imphal Plain). Giffard supported Slim's strategy. Scoones switched Roberts' 23rd Division with Gracey's 20th Division hoping that the latter would achieve more when directed on Ukhrul.

Mutaguchi ordered General Sato to make another attack in conjunction with 15th Division, but Sato, hopelessly short of ammunition and supplies, with his men literally starving and his flank threatened, took no notice of these orders and started to retire to the Chindwin. For this he was relieved of his command in June. Yanagida of 33rd Division had been dismissed in May and Yamauchi, commanding 15th Division, was dismissed at about the same time as Sato. This wholesale riddance of his three divisional commanders by Mutaguchi was unprecedented and helped to hasten the decline in morale of his troops.

The advance on Ukhrul was delayed by fierce storms. Perowne's brigade, spread out in columns, was held up by bad weather and small pockets of resistance. Gracey's 20th Division, although operating along a thinly metalled road which was not so vulnerable to wet weather, was also held up.

Grover's 2nd Division had fought its way down the Imphal road from Kohima and on 22nd June the junction was made between the two corps at Milestone 109, only just north of the Imphal Plain. Stopford had advanced seventy miles from Kohima, but Scoones had only managed less than ten miles up hill out of the plain. This led to recriminations between the two corps; it would seem that Scoones had not pressed north with sufficient vigour and had waited 'like a maiden tied to a tree for a knight to rescue her' as one XXXIII Corps officer put it.

However the British attempt to encircle 15th and 31st Division by the capture of Ukhrul failed. These two divisions had realised the importance of Ukhrul and fought determinedly to keep this corridor open until their depleted divisions had passed through. From 3rd to 7th July the Japanese had held grimly onto the Ukhrul area. Organised resistance ceased on the 8th and 23rd Brigade and 20th Division met each other. Their orders were the hot pursuit of the enemy retreating towards the Chindwin. But, as the Official History relates: 'There was no need to carry out Giffard's suggestion of pressing the pursuit to the Chindwin, since a great proportion of the men of 15th and 31st Divisions who had survived the battle (Kohima-Imphal) were found dead and dying of disease and exhaustion. Bodies, guns, vehicles, and equipment lay rotting and rusting along the quagmire that had once been the tracks from Ukhrul, scenes of horror which compelled pity, for it was obvious that many of the dead had been sick and wounded men, who had dropped and died of starvation or been drowned in the ooze that filled every rut and pothole.'

So, as the monsoon broke, ended the great U-Go offensive, this so-called 'March on Delhi'.

It had been an administratively impossible task for the Japanese which relied on the troops of IV Corps not fighting and giving up their dumps of supplies. Once they formed to fight around these supplies, and the airfields which brought them relief, the Japanese offensive was doomed. Everything had depended, as it had ever done in this area of the world, on the morale of the troops, and on which side would break first. Slim had always realised this and his main task had been to keep up the morale not only of his men, but his weary corps and divisional commanders and urge them on to battle. Having fought under such conditions himself, he could speak their own language and understand their problems, so it was no mere exhortation from on high. Slim always led from the ruck and not from the touchline. He epitomised determination, resolution, courage, durability and strength. All commanders have, to a certain extent, to be actors as they are always watched. Slim, although possessing a more devious brain than those who did not know him intimately credited him with, knew and understood the cut of his own figure, his prominent jaw and determined silent stance, and used them to their best advantage.

Slim had won his greatest battle. Out of a total strength of nearly 100,000 men who started off on Mutaguchi's U-Go offensive the Japanese lost 53,000 of whom 30,000 died. Most of those who escaped suffered from minor wounds, disease and malnutrition. The two northern divisions, with their precarious communications, suffered the worst, and both 15th and 31st Japanese Divisions could be written off as fighting units until such time as they could refit and obtain reinforcements. 33rd Division, based on roads, withdrew in better order, but was still harassed by the RAF who followed them inexorably along the roads and probably caused almost as much damage to vehicles

The Ukhrul road from Imphal

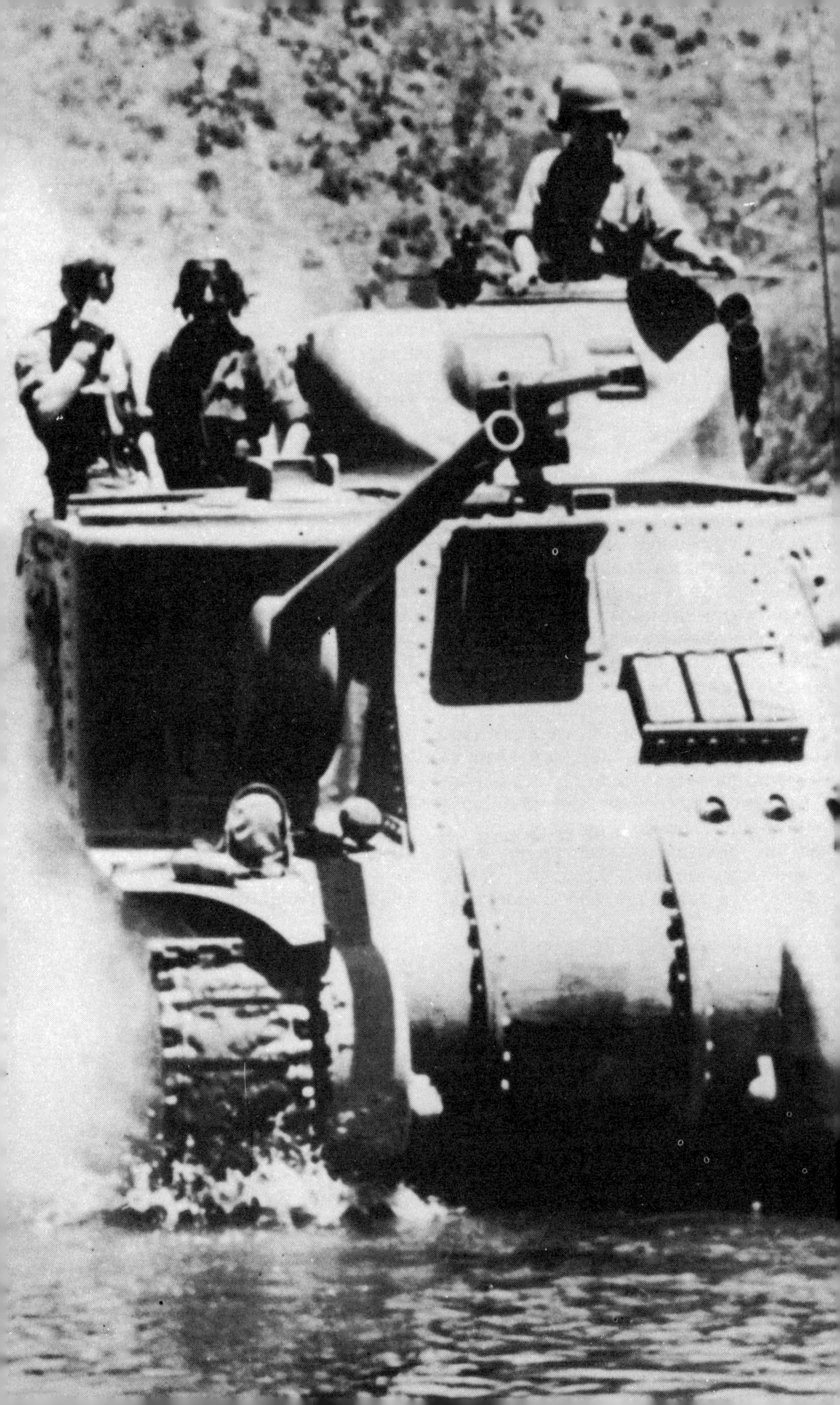

and equipment as ever the infantry divisions had done.

Slim estimated that the Japanese losses including the Arakan were as high as 90,000, but the figure appears too large when we consider the resistance they were able to put up later in the campaign. However Japanese historians have repeatedly admitted that it was their greatest land defeat to date, possibly only surpassed by the American reconquest of the Philippines and the Russian incursion into Manchuria at the very end of the war. Fourteenth Army losses, including Arakan, were 24,000 of which 4,000 were at Kohima, 12,000 at Imphal and the remaining 8,000 during XXXIII Corps' advance, and in the Arakan.

Twice Slim had underestimated the strength of attack, in the Arakan and at Imphal. But in each case, with the great help and cooperation of his superiors, Giffard and Mountbatten, and the ever willing air forces who would always support anyone who wanted to fight, he was immediately able to draw on large reinforcements which, when properly deployed, could overwhelm the enemy by numbers, armour and fire power.

Slim had achieved his stated object of letting the Japanese bash their heads against a wall when far from their bases so that he could defeat them on ground of his own choosing. The fact that the Japanese did much better than he expected did not, on the whole, make him lose his nerve at each crucial point. He maintained a steady calm and did not heed the clamour for more action or the strident cries of alarm from British and Indian politicians and civilians, but kept steady on his course.

His first small victory in the Arakan had made him much more self confident, so that he could weather the much greater threat at Imphal with aplomb. His long years of defeat were ended. He could now look confidently to the future.

British tank north of Imphal

The Blackpool plan

General Wingate's British, West African and Gurkha troops await emplanement to fly to Broadway

Having discussed Slim's role in the Arakan and Imphal battles, we must now go back to look briefly at the Chindits and Stilwell's forces, which were also under his overall command. In accordance with the Quebec plan, Wingate's Chindits were to operate south of the Mogaung-Myitkyina line, and cut all communications to the Japanese 18th and 56th Divisions facing the American-Chinese armies.

After losing 23rd Brigade to XXXIII Corps, Wingate had five brigades each of four battalions under his command. One of these, 16th Brigade marched into Burma, while the others flew in from the night of 5th March onwards. By the end of March, they had placed an almost impregnable block across the main Japanese communications to the north. A 77th Brigade detachment, later called Morris Force, had blocked the Bhamo-Myitkyina road, and no Japanese traffic could use the Irrawaddy river. The Mandalay-Myitkyina railway was also cut. A formidable defensive position was established at White City, on the railway, as a honey-pot to attract the Japanese offensive spirit; vicious fighting took place there from 6th to 18th April, in which the six battalion attacking force with its artillery was virtually destroyed.

Wingate did not live to see this success, as he had been killed in a flying accident on 24th March: a deep tragedy for the British army. Slim chose the senior brigade commander, Lentaigne, as his successor, and John Masters took over Lentaigne's 111th Brigade.

The Japanese had been taken almost completely by surprise by the landings. After the first Chindit operation they had expected a similar foray, but like Slim, their Area Commander underestimated its possible strength. For some time the Japanese were unaware of the size of the Chindit force, and sent individual battalions against it which were defeated in turn. Altogether, eleven Japanese battalions were engaged and defeated by the Chindits in this period. These were drawn mainly from the units protecting the coast of Burma against possible seaborne landings, for once the Japanese realised the size of the Chindit landing, they knew that Mountbatten could not afford to land on the coast that season as well as by air in north Burma. One battalion was drawn from each of the divisions facing the Chinese, and from 15th Division at Imphal.

Slim's role in these events was ambivalent. He had not been keen on the Chindit operation, and most of the planning for it had been made without his full knowledge. It was only Mountbatten's insistence on the operation,

77th (Chindit) Brigade's White City Block on the main Japanese rail link leading to the Chinese-American front

and Stilwell's adamant demand for the fulfillment of the promise which the British had made at Quebec, that forced the fly-in to take place. Slim, most unfortunately, always looked on these operations in north Burma with disfavour, and tended to denigrate them. It was also natural for him somewhat to resent an individualistic commander operating on his front in a flamboyant manner which upset his own generals. He appreciated how much Wingate had achieved by his successes for the morale of Fourteenth Army. But there was also some counterproductive effect on the morale of the men of IV Corps, who felt that they had been neglected after holding the line for two whole years. Wingate had acted almost independently of

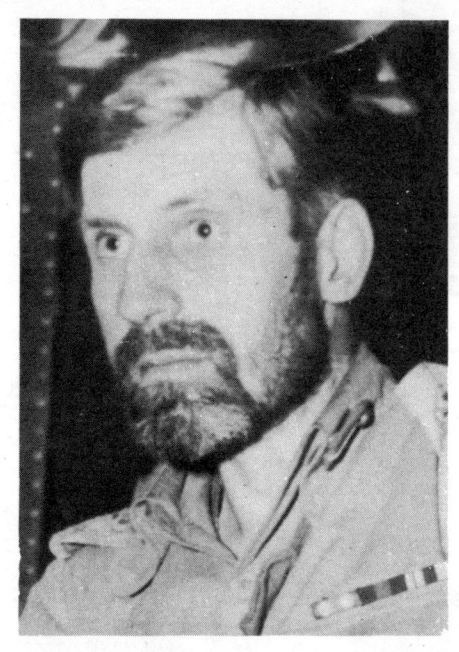

Major-General Orde Wingate in a mule-carrying Dakota aircraft just before his death

Major-General Lentaigne, Wingate's successor

WACO gliders land

Fourteenth Army, although Slim had had to bring him to heel more than once; with Lentaigne, a fellow Gurkha, in command, Slim felt that he could exercise closer control.

On the other hand once the operation took place, Slim supported the Chindits, with their lost leader, throughout, and nursed Lentaigne as Wingate's successor. Although severely pressed for aircraft, he never once allowed the Chindits to go short, and stubbornly maintained his promise to Stilwell that the Chindits would be used primarily to support his advance in the north, and not be deflected to support IV Corps at Imphal.

Shortly before his death, Wingate had suggested to Slim that he should switch his whole effort west to cut all communications over the Chindwin by manning the eastern banks of the Chindwin behind Mutaguchi. Slim, although attracted to the idea, turned it down on two grounds. First he thought that the dry open waterless country from Kalewa south was unsuitable for Chindit operations. Secondly he felt that he must keep faith with Stilwell and the decision at the Quebec Conference that the primary objective of the 1944 season was to open the route to China. Wingate, who was determined not to loosen his grip on the Japanese communications to north Burma, pointed out that Stilwell had stopped his advance and that the Chinese on the Salween front were supine due to the Japanese threat against the road and air communications in the Assam Valley. It was of little use, he said, to cut the communications of a force which was not fighting at the end of them because it could live on its reserves and local produce.

But Slim was adamant. The British had promised to cut and keep cut these communications to the north, and they would abide by their word. Two days later Wingate was dead.

This was a loyal, courageous and

INDAW AREA
21st March – 1st April 1944

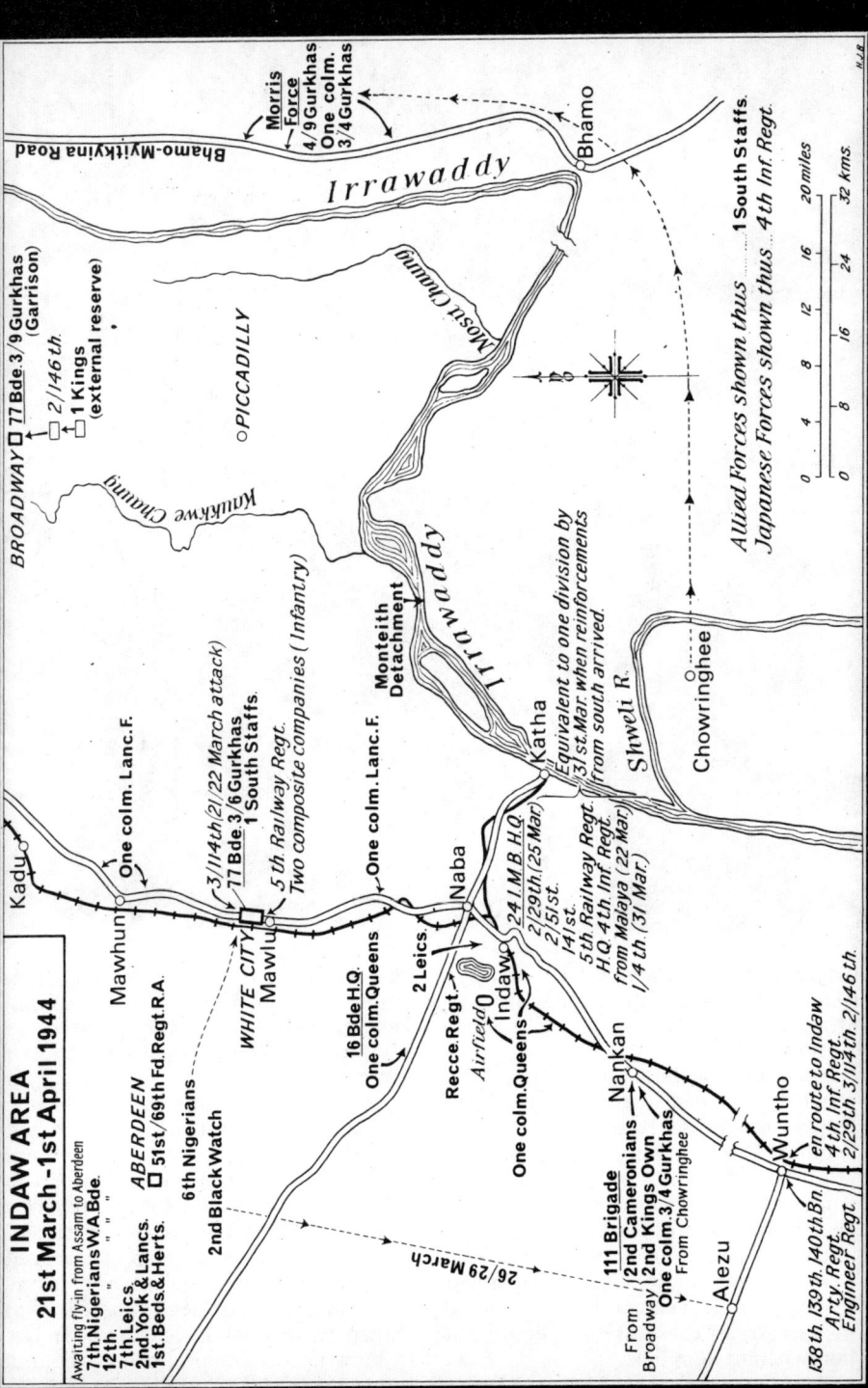

Awaiting fly-in from Assam to Aberdeen
7th Nigerians W A Bde.
12th.
7th Leics.
2nd York & Lancs.
1st Beds & Herts.

ABERDEEN ☐ 51st/69th Fd.Regt.R.A.

Allied Forces shown thus ——— 1 South Staffs.
Japanese Forces shown thus ——— 4th Inf. Regt.

Scale: 0 4 8 12 16 20 miles / 0 8 16 24 32 kms.

Morris Force 4/9 Gurkhas, One colm. 3/4 Gurkhas

Bhamo

Irrawaddy

Bhamo-Myitkyina Road

BROADWAY ☐ 77 Bde. 3/9 Gurkhas (Garrison)
2/146th
1 Kings (external reserve)

○ PICCADILLY

Mosit (Chaung)

Kauhkwe Chaung

Kadu ○
One colm. Lanc.F.
Mawhun ○

3/114th (21/22 March attack)
77 Bde. 3/6 Gurkhas 1 South Staffs.
WHITE CITY ☐
Mawlu ○ — 5th Railway Regt. Two composite companies (Infantry)

One colm. Lanc.F.

Monteith Detachment

Naba
16 Bde H.Q.
One colm. Queens
2 Leics.

24 I M B H.Q. (25 Mar)
2/29th
2/51st
141st.
Katha — Equivalent to one division by 31st Mar. when reinforcements from south arrived.
5th Railway Regt. H.Q. 4th Inf. Regt. from Malaya (22 Mar)
1/4 th. (31 Mar)

Recce Regt. ○ Airfield
Indaw
One colm. Queens

6th Nigerians
2nd Black Watch

Nankan

Chowringhee

Shweli R.

111 Brigade
From 2nd Cameronians
Broadway 2nd Kings Own
One colm. 3/4 Gurkhas
From Chowringhee

Wuntho
en route to Indaw
4th Inf. Regt.
2/29th 3/114th 2/146th

Alezu

138th 139th 140th Bn.
Arty. Regt.
Engineer Regt.

26/29 March

Brigadier Michael Calvert, Lieutenant-Colonel Shaw and Major Lumley at Mogaung

honourable decision by Slim, who must have been sorely tempted to relieve the pressure on his troops at Imphal. The decision may have been slightly influenced by the fact that Slim did not want to feel bounden to the Chindits for victory over the Japanese which he hoped to achieve. Now that he had XXXIII Corps under his command, eventual victory should be certain as the Japanese could not last without supplies.

Even so, while the Chindits' main role was to help the American-Chinese force forward to Mogaung and Myitkyina and open a route to China, their operations also greatly assisted IV Corps in their resistance to the Japanese attack.

111th Brigade, which operated south of Indaw, and 14th Brigade which had landed at Aberdeen, had between them cut the land communications of the Japanese 31st and 15th Divisions attacking Kohima and north of Imphal. They had also destroyed dumps east of the Chindwin and, in one case, isolated a large quantity of transport between Homalin and Indaw by blowing a number of bridges behind them. From the air angle, the Chindit invasion drew off half the effort of the

Japanese 5th Air Division, which left their troops across the Chindwin woefully short of supplies and support.

In April the invasion was to have an even more serious effect. Mutaguchi had been relying on 53rd Division, now arriving in Burma, as a reserve to assist him to take Imphal. Now Burma Area Army deflected the whole of 53rd Division to clear up the airborne forces. Mutaguchi complained later, 'If I had had only one regiment of 53rd Division, I could have taken Imphal and opened the route to the Assam Valley.'

In May there was a major change of plan for the Chindits. Lentaigne believed erroneously that supplies were infiltrating between the blocks at Aberdeen, White City and Broadway, where in any case the airstrips would soon become flooded and useless in the approaching monsoon. For both these reasons, he decided to shift his area of operations northwards. The exhausted 16th Brigade was flown out, and the other forces moved up towards Myitkyina, Mogaung and the Indawggyi Lake, with 111th Brigade forming a new block at Blackpool.

Stilwell was violently opposed to this plan as being a blatant departure from the agreements laid down in the Quebec Conference. He feared that all this manoeuvring would allow Japanese reinforcements to reach Mogaung-Myitkyina (which they did). He wanted the Chindits to continue to operate in the area which they knew and dominated. He feared the effect of a withdrawal on the Burmese population which had been becoming friendly and he did not want the Chindits to become mixed up in his tactical battle. He had his own 'Merrill's Marauders' available for short range penetration. He registered his objections most vigorously to Mountbatten, Slim and the Chiefs of Staff in Washington.

Slim instructed Lentaigne to approach Stilwell but he was snubbed. Mountbatten prevailed upon Slim, who was busy with the implications of the Imphal battle, to see Stilwell. With his tact and charm turned full on, and relying on their past friendship and identity of purpose, Slim managed to convince Stilwell that Lentaigne's plan was based on logistical necessities. As an anodyne he offered to put the whole Chindit force

Merrill's Marauders on the Ledo Road

of five brigades at the disposal of Stilwell and under his command. This was to cause more trouble later as Stilwell had little knowledge of what they had already done or of their capabilities. Slim, in spite of trying to understand and support the Chindits, never liked their role or methods of operation and was glad to have one less formation with which to concern himself. So Stilwell agreed to the Blackpool plan and to take command of the Chindits.

The remaining Chindit brigades were soon involved in very heavy fighting with 53rd Division, which went straight into action against them on arriving in Burma, sending only a single battalion to help Mutaguchi on the Chindwin. 111th Brigade was forced to evacuate the Blackpool block, after inflicting and receiving heavy losses. Calvert's 77th Brigade attacked northwards, suffering 1,000 casualties in three weeks of muddy monsoon fighting before capturing Mogaung. A regiment of Stilwell's 38th Chinese Division joined at the last moment so that the Allies entered Mogaung together on 25th June. This was the first town in Burma to be recaptured. The fighting strength of 77th Brigade was now down to little more than 300.

Stilwell, meanwhile, had been inching forward by a series of hooks around the regiments of 18th Division opposing him. These hooks were carried out by Merrill's Marauders, who had trained with the Chindits, and who were the only all-American ground fighting unit on the mainland of Asia. They were excellent material, but Stilwell, by force of circumstances, used them again and again until by August they were finished. He used them in one last coup, brilliant in its planning and execution, where they marched over the rugged hills and seized the airfield at Myitkyina, a form of 'island hopping' on land which Wingate had dreamed of. A Chinese division was quickly flown in but not before about 3,000 Japanese had dug themselves in a practically impregnable position in the town of Myitkyina from which it took two and a half months and 30,000 Allied troops to eliminate them.

Finally, by August, when Myitkyina fell and the Chinese moved south of Mogaung, the northern campaign was nearing completion. From July the Chindits were being flown out and being relieved by the British 36th Division flown up from the Arakan. Only the Chindit mules remained to help 36th Division forward down the railway. The Chinese armies on the Salween at last made a massive attack and swept the weakened Japanese 56th Division away south of Bhamo. By September the objectives of the Quebec Conference had been gained. Mogaung and Myitkyina, with an area south of them, were in the Allies' hands and shortly the oil pipe line and road to China were opened. Myitkyina airfield could be used as an air staging post, and the dangerous 'Hump' route to China, although still used, could follow a less arduous flight path.

In addition, the Allies were now firmly installed on the Irrawaddy Plain as the British 36th Division advanced down to Indaw and towards the summer capital of Maymyo where the Burma Area Army Headquarters was situated. In the central front Kalemyo on the Chindwin, the base for the U-Go offensive, was not to fall until 13th November, so the Stilwell-Chindit northern offensive had broken through the mountains to a position threatening Mutaguchi's right flank and rear long before Fourteenth Army had crossed the Chindwin.

The American-Chinese-Chindit operation had knocked out the key stone of the arch or the Japanese defence. But this had not happened without some intense friction among the higher command. Perhaps anything worth doing well is not accomplished without friction, in which case it should be accepted as a by-product of an alliance fighting a war.

SITUATION at 4th – 24th April 1944

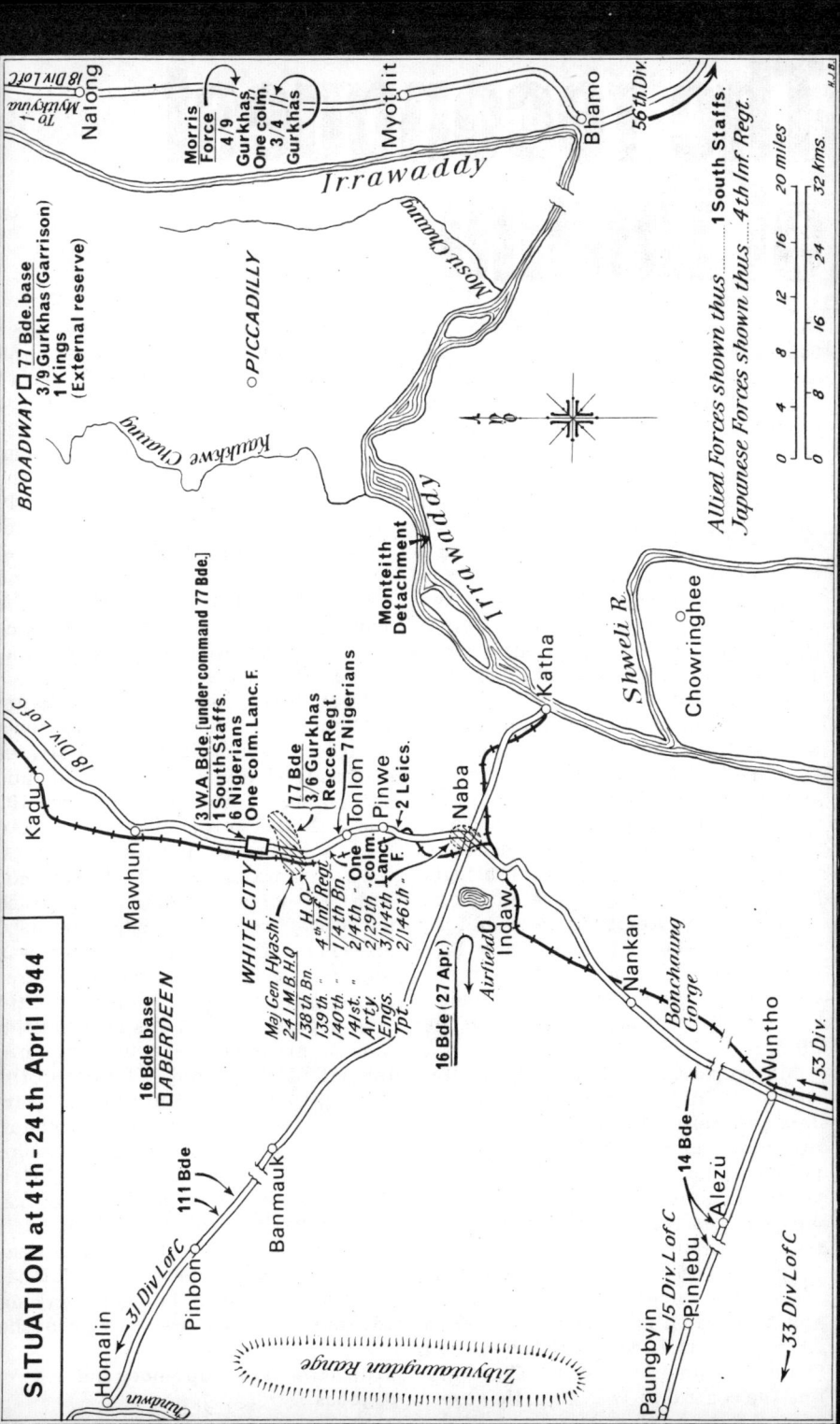

BROADWAY ☐ 77 Bde base
3/9 Gurkhas (Garrison)
1 Kings
(External reserve)

Morris Force
4/9 Gurkhas, One colm.
3/4 Gurkhas

To Myitkyina
Nalong
Myothit
Bhamo
56th Div.
18 Div L of C

Irrawaddy
Mosé Chaung
○ PICCADILLY
Kaukkwe Chaung

Allied Forces shown thus ——— 1 South Staffs.
Japanese Forces shown thus ═══ 4th Inf. Regt.

0 4 8 12 16 20 miles
0 8 16 24 32 kms.

Monteith Detachment

Irrawaddy
Shweli R.
Katha
Chowringhee

16 Bde base ☐ ABERDEEN

Kadu — Mawhun — **WHITE CITY** — Tonlon — Pinwe — Naba

3 W.A. Bde. [under command 77 Bde.]
1 South Staffs.
6 Nigerians
One colm. Lanc. F.

77 Bde
3/6 Gurkhas
Recce. Regt.
7 Nigerians
2 Leics.

Maj Gen Hyashi H.Q.
24 I.M.B.H.Q.   4th Inf Regt.
138th Bn   1/4th Bn
139th "   2/4th — One colm.
140th "   2/29th Lanc. F.
14st. "   3/114th
Arty   2/146th
Engs.
Tpt.

16 Bde (27 Apr.)
Airfield ○ Indaw
Nankan
Bonchaung Gorge
Wuntho
53 Div.

111 Bde
Banmauk
Pinbon
31 Div L of C
Homalin
Ouwwu

14 Bde
Alezu
Pinlebu
Paungbyin
15 Div L of C
33 Div L of C

Zibyutaungpin Range

H.J.B.

The reconquest of Burma

On 3rd June, nearly three weeks before the fall of Mogaung and Myitkyina, and the junction of XXXIII and IV Corps, Mountbatten received a directive from the Combined Chiefs of Staff, Washington which emphasised that the main importance of the campaign in Burma was to get supplies through to China and make that route safe.

This meant that Mountbatten's main object was not necessarily the conquest of Burma, but to open the oil route from Ledo in Assam to China. He was to receive no landing craft and was forced to make the best use of what he had.

On the Imphal front, Mountbatten wanted Giffard's Eleventh Army Group to move on after the relief of Imphal and pursue the enemy over the Chindwin. On 9th June Giffard was ordered to clear the enemy from the west bank of the Chindwin and to make bridgeheads across it before the monsoon stopped in September. He would be given two more divisions, the 19th Indian and the 11th East African but would lose the British 36th Division to Stilwell eventually, to replace the Chindits.

Giffard passed his orders on to Slim who certainly intended to give the Japanese no respite and who ordered Stopford and Scoones to carry out a pursuit of 15th and 31st Divisions with their own nine divisions and, if possible, to destroy them before they reached the Chindwin.

The Japanese, in turn, realised that the 'U-Go' offensive had now failed and Mutaguchi ordered his Fifteenth Army to withdraw to the Zibyu Taungdan range between the Chindwin and the central railway line. However, he still wanted his better equipped 33rd Division to hold a southern flank from the Zibyu Taungdan Range to Kalewa and Kalemyo covering the Gangaw Valley.

By 31st July 23rd Division had recaptured Tamu and was nearing the Chindwin. 20th Division had slowly advanced over difficult country towards Homalin. 5th Division had relieved the battle-weary 17th and were advancing south along the Tiddim Road against minor resistance and the East African Division was concentrating at Imphal.

After the relief of Imphal Slim, without letting his forces pause for a breather, reorganised his divisions so that fresh divisions could continue the pursuit. Scoones's IV Corps HQ and 17th and 20th Divisions, who had been holding the line for two years, were withdrawn to India for a refit. 50th Parachute Brigade was also withdrawn so that it could be used elsewhere. Unfortunately Slim was unsympathetic to any form of parachute operation and it did not obtain any opportunity on his front. Slim moved his own headquarters into Imphal. He ordered XXXIII Corps under Stopford to continue the pursuit of the Japanese 33rd Division southwards with British 2nd, Indian 5th and 20th and East African 11th Divisions which now formed his corps.

Mountbatten had ordered Stilwell to clear the area south of Mogaung-Myitkyina as far south as Katha-Bhamo, with the final object of taking advantage of this break-in onto the

British troops mop up among the pagodas

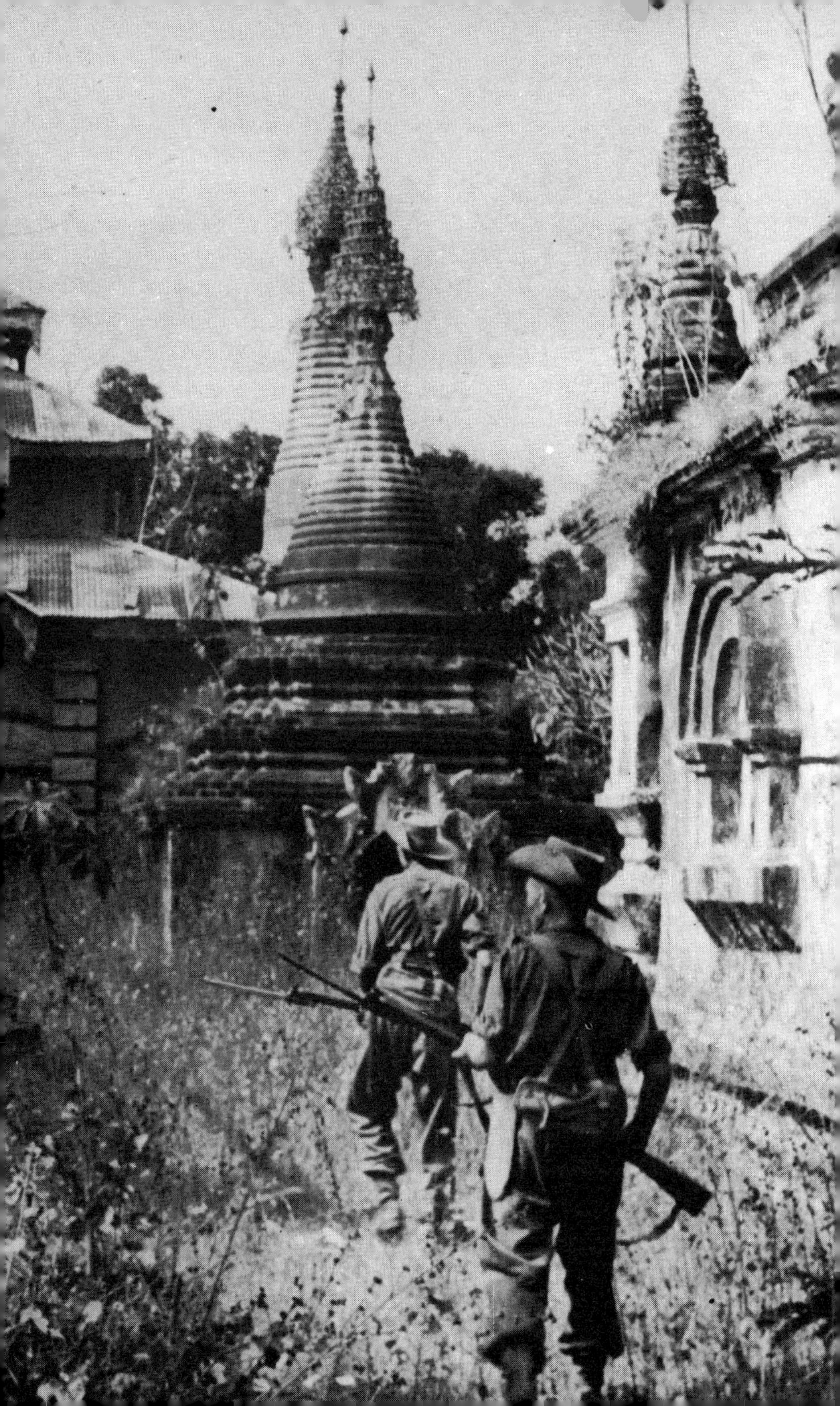

A Japanese position under shell fire on the Tamu road

Irrawaddy Plain by forming a line from Kalewa to Lashio.

He wanted IV and XXXIII Corps to cross the Chindwin to the area Ye-U and Shwebo and go on to Mandalay. This operation was named 'Capital'. He also naturally hankered after a landing to capture Rangoon and so box the Japanese armies in Burma, but he did not, as yet, have the landing craft available. However he set his planners on to this operation which was named 'Dracula'.

Giffard wanted Slim to awaken the moribund Arakan theatre again to try and take Akyab, that sterile objective which had so long evaded capture.

Due to divergences of opinion between the American and British Chiefs of Staff, Mountbatten could not obtain orders until eventually Churchill and Roosevelt met with their Chiefs of Staff at the Octagon Conference in Quebec on 11th-16th September. Mountbatten was then given his orders. First of all, he was to ensure the security of the existing air supply route to China including the air staging post at Myitkyina, and to open a land route as well. Secondly, he was at last told that his objective should be to recapture Burma at the earliest date. The operation 'Capital' was approved as it assisted him to attain his first object, the protection of the air route to China and the opening of a land route. Dracula was also approved but should be accomplished, if possible, before the 15th March 1945. If it could not be mounted before the 1945 monsoon, 'Capital' should be exploited as far as possible to conquer Burma by land.

These orders were passed on to Slim as far as they were relevant. In the meantime he was driving Stopford on

General Stilwell and Chinese Colonel Lee examine captured Japanese weapons and gas masks

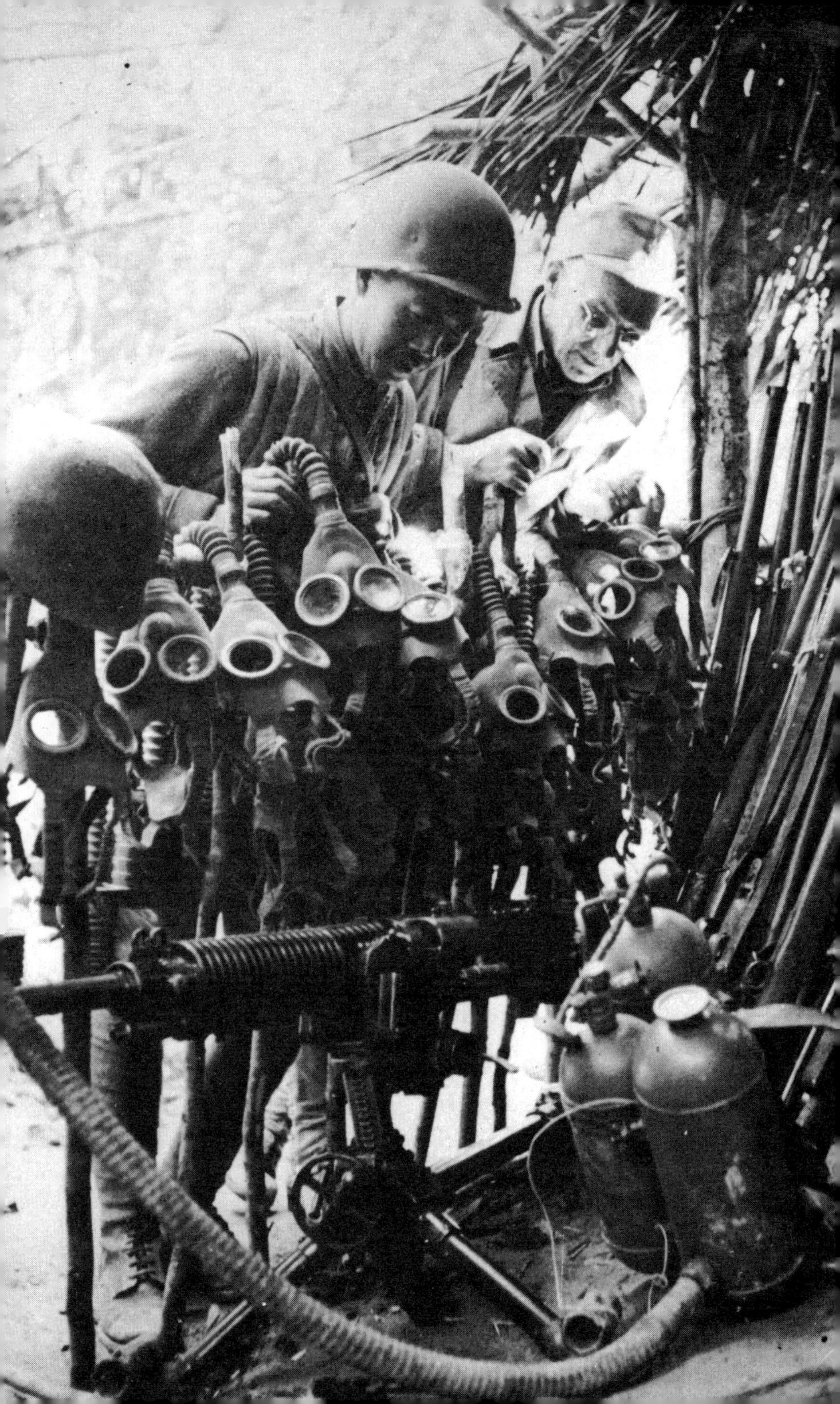

to recapture the Chindwin crossing places at Kalewa and Sittaung. He also ordered pursuit down the Tiddim road, mainly because it was there and it would widen the front of his attack and confuse the Japanese as to his immediate objective which was Kalewa.

But this was at the height of the monsoon when it was easier to give orders than carry them out. Diseases of all kinds decimated the troops however many precautions were taken. Flooded streams and rivers held up the advance and destroyed bridges behind the advance guards. Landslides blocked the road, and sometimes a whole road formation would disappear down the hillside. Aircraft could not resupply amongst the cloud-enshrouded mountains. Mules and fourwheel-drive jeeps with chains were the only forms of transport which could master the mud. Japanese 33rd Division, although itself rent with disease and lack of supplies, could put up a stubborn resistance against the movement of these four divisions who often could only advance on a one-jeep front.

So it was not until 13th November as the monsoon ceased that the East African 11th and 5th Division met at Kalemyo. The Chindwin had, however, been crossed at Mawlaik and Sittaung which widened the front and by 2nd December Kalewa was

Allied leaders confer in Quebec

captured and a 1,150-foot Bailey Bridge on pontoons soon spanned the Chindwin. A road route was open into the heart of north Burma by Christmas, by which time the weather was dry.

The Japanese forces had now been reorganised into three armies. Mutaguchi had been dismissed. Thirty-third Army facing north consisting of the battered 18th and 56th Divisions was still opposing Stilwell's Chinese, the Yunnan Chinese armies from the Salween and British 36th Division on the long line from Lashio to Mandalay. Fifteenth Army with the remnants of 15th and 31st Divisions, the better equipped 33rd Division, and 53rd Division which had received a battering at Blackpool and Mogaung, faced Stopford's XXXIII Corps along the Irrawaddy line from Mandalay to Pakkoku, with one division in reserve at Meiktila. Twenty-eighth Army consisting of 55th Division which had so ably defended Akyab and 54th Division plus one regiment, defended the Arakan and the coast line as far as Rangoon and the Irrawaddy Delta, with some reserves at the Yenangyaung oil field area. The remaining two divisions were Area Army reserve and left mobile on the Rangoon-Mandalay railway area so that they could be quickly switched to any

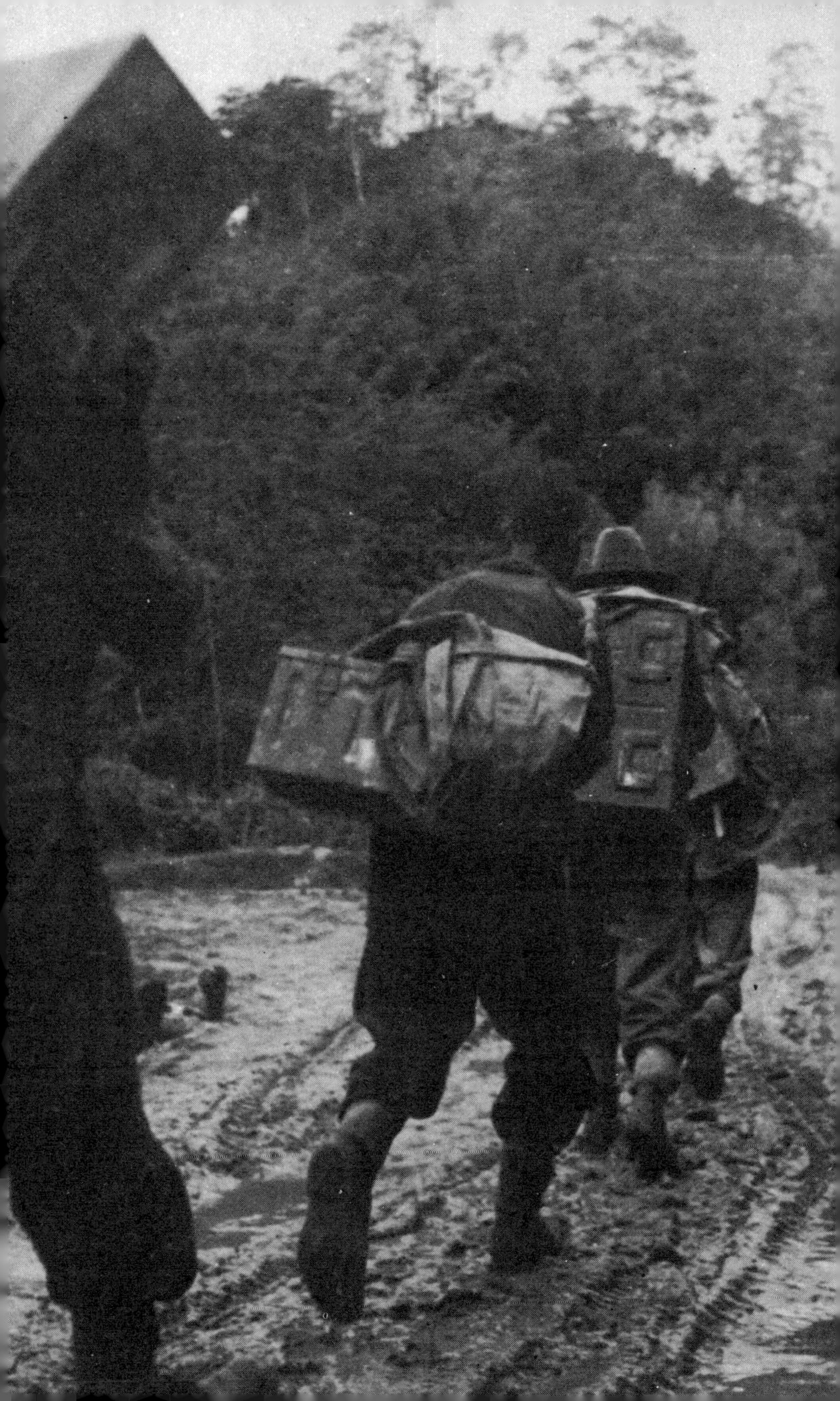

Right: Gurkhas hump ammunition from an air drop. *Above:* Royal Engineers and Indian Sappers and Miners construct a Bailey pontoon bridge over the Chindwin near Kalewa. *Below:* Man-power where horse-power has failed

Sir William and Lady Slim at Imphal

threatened front. Now that the Allies held the initiative, the Japanese in turn had to spread out their forces over this 1,000-mile front. Their divisions had all taken a severe battering, and reinforcements, new equipment and supplies from distant Japan, across the American-dominated South Pacific, were meagre.

After their experience with the Chindits all armies and the Burma Area Army kept substantial reserves in case of further airborne attacks.

In spite of orders to capture certain identified objectives like Mandalay, Slim firmly adhered to his belief that his first aim must be to defeat the Japanese armies and that all else would follow. He would not be mesmerised by the names of towns, but would pursue, encircle and destroy the enemy wherever he was, using the maximum amount of manoeuvre, deception and guile to achieve this result. It was a very confident and mature army commander who now stood up to his superiors. Slim had gained immensely in stature and self confidence since his orders and steadfastness had achieved victories in the Arakan and Imphal.

But Slim's effort was now severely limited by administrative considerations. It was 400 miles from the

Assam railhead at Dimapur to a new railhead in Burma at Shwebo. These 400 miles were across some of the worst country in the world. His first task had to be to transform this thin thread into an all-weather route, or he would be caught without communications on the Burma plain by the next monsoon.

The narrow umbilical cord to India would limit the size of his operations and the number of divisions he could deploy unless he relied further on air supply. He calculated that he could only deploy a maximum of $4\frac{2}{3}$ divisions including two tank brigades for operations on the plain of Burma. The advantages of capturing Akyab and Ramree islands off the Arakan coast would be that these islands could provide excellent airbases for air supply into central Burma now that the Imphal and Assam bases were becoming too far away and uneconomic. So Slim decided that his XV Corps under Christison would have to capture these bases with any landing craft available.

But this capture of Akyab was not to be his responsibility. In November General Giffard placed Christison's XV Corps and the Line of Communication area directly under his own Eleventh Army Group Command in order to relieve Slim of responsibility for his rear areas, and to let him get on with the fighting at the front.

Many months previously, when the Chinese-American capture of Kamaing, north of Mogaung, seemed remote, Stilwell had agreed to serve under Eleventh Army Group with the stipulation that when Kamaing was captured he should come under direct command of the Supreme Commander. On 16th June, on the capture of Kamaing, he had claimed this heritage and so Slim had lost control over Stilwell's Northern Combat Area Command which included at that time, the Chindits, and then 36th Division who replaced them. Mountbatten, consequently, asked for the appointment of a Commander-in-Chief Land Forces so that he could deal with only one army commander.

So, also in November 1944, Eleventh Army Group HQ was abolished and a new HQ Allied Land Forces South East Asia (ALFSEA) was formed to command all land operations against the Japanese in Burma. The long, successful, and amicable partnership of Giffard and Slim was broken up, and Giffard returned to Britain. Lieutenant-General Oliver Leese, a guardsman who had commanded Eighth Army in Italy, was brought in to command ALFSEA.

The Italian front had never been more than 130 miles wide and easy to control, with good communications. An army commander could call in his divisional commanders to dinner without making them desert their command for more than a few hours. Leese tried this in Burma and never realised that the divisional commander had to travel on horseback, jeep, light aircraft and hired car for a period of two or three days in order to come to dinner and be given a farewell 'Glad to meet you' at the end. It took a long time for Leese to settle down and appreciate the size, remoteness and constitutional make-up of his command. Giffard, who hated flying as he had had so many accidents, always flew forward everywhere, making reports and handing copies with suggestions only to Slim. Morale was always the main factor on both sides under these terrible conditions, and it was essential that a commander should be seen with a rifle over his shoulder in the front line. Slim, Stilwell and Giffard were excellent at this essential duty which is taught to every subaltern, and took great physical and mental pains to carry it out over vast stretches of thinly held country, but Oliver Leese at first tried to command by remote control and from the drawing board. A battalion commander who thinks that he can command a battalion from a coal cellar and does not visit his forward platoons daily is wrong, however skilful he may be. He will never get the troops to fight outstandingly well for him. So it is with an army or corps commander. He must be seen to be believed, especially at the beginning of a campaign when the troops are raw and at the end when they are weary. Therefore, he must have a good physique as well as some brains. But his greatest asset is sensitivity, so that he is a receiving-transmitting set, responsive to the feelings, often unexpressed, of his men and thus being able to convert these responses into orders worded so that they will be glad to carry them out. As Slim has shown in his essays on Courage and other subjects, he had this sensitivity and responsiveness developed to a high degree – he was not called 'Uncle Bill' for nothing – and it stood him in better stead than academic and technical brilliance.

After Imphal Slim wanted pursuers, so he reorganised the top echelons of his command and sought men of dash, questing spirit and thrustful determination to lead his divisions. He appointed Lieutenant-General Messervy, who had been overrun in the Western Desert and in the Arakan and had come up smiling and fighting like a wild cat each time, to take Scoones's place commanding a reconstituted IV Corps. Major-General Evans, who had had immense experience in the Middle East, in the Arakan and at Imphal both as a commander and operational staff officer, now commanded 7th Division. Major-General

General Slim with Major-General Fowkes, commander of 11th East African Division, cross the Chindwin by ferry

after the victories of Imphal and Arakan. They were spruce, streamlined, could move fast needing few orders, knew how to look after their tail, had the measure of their enemy and his tactics, understood how to use to the best advantage air supply and the tremendous strength of close support bombing, and knew how to curl up their strength into a coiled spring ready for the next advance.

Much of the praise for this transformation should go to General Auchinleck, C-in-C India, who was responsible for all training of the Indian Army and the British and African armies in India. He was a wise man and had planned to raise a new model Indian Army. By mid-1944 his policy was paying sound dividends.

The Japanese plan was to try to hold a line north of Shwebo-Ye-U and over the Chindwin to just south of Kalemyo, which the British had captured, whilst they reorganised their defeated armies. Slim's plan was not to leave them in peace.

Messervy's IV Corps was to cross the Zibyu-Taungdan Range from the Sittaung bridgehead, capture Pinlebu and then turn south, still west of the Irrawaddy to capture the road, rail and airfield complex of Shwebo in the dry belt. 36th Division, who had advanced down the railway, would cover their left flank.

The Lushai Brigade and the 28th East African Brigade were to move down the Gangaw Valley from Kalemyo as a preliminary, and once the general advance had started, East African 11th Division would be flown out to India to relieve the supply position.

Stopford's 2nd and 20th Divisions were to move across the Chindwin at Kalewa to capture Ye-U (near Shwebo) and Monywa.

Crossing the Chindwin at Sittaung

Rees, a dynamic Welshman who led his men from the front, and from the front only, commanded 19th Division. Messervy also had 268th Brigade and 255th Tank Brigade under command.

It will be remembered that Slim had calculated that he could only maintain $4\frac{2}{3}$ divisions in the field on the plains of Burma. So Stopford's XXXIII Corps was also to be trimmed for speed. 2nd (British) Division had a new divisional commander, Major-General Nicholson but that reliable old campaigner who had done so well at Imphal, Major-General Gracey, still commanded 20th Division. Stopford also had a tank brigade (254th) under his command.

These divisions were unrecognizable when compared with the inexperienced divisions of 1943. They had confidence

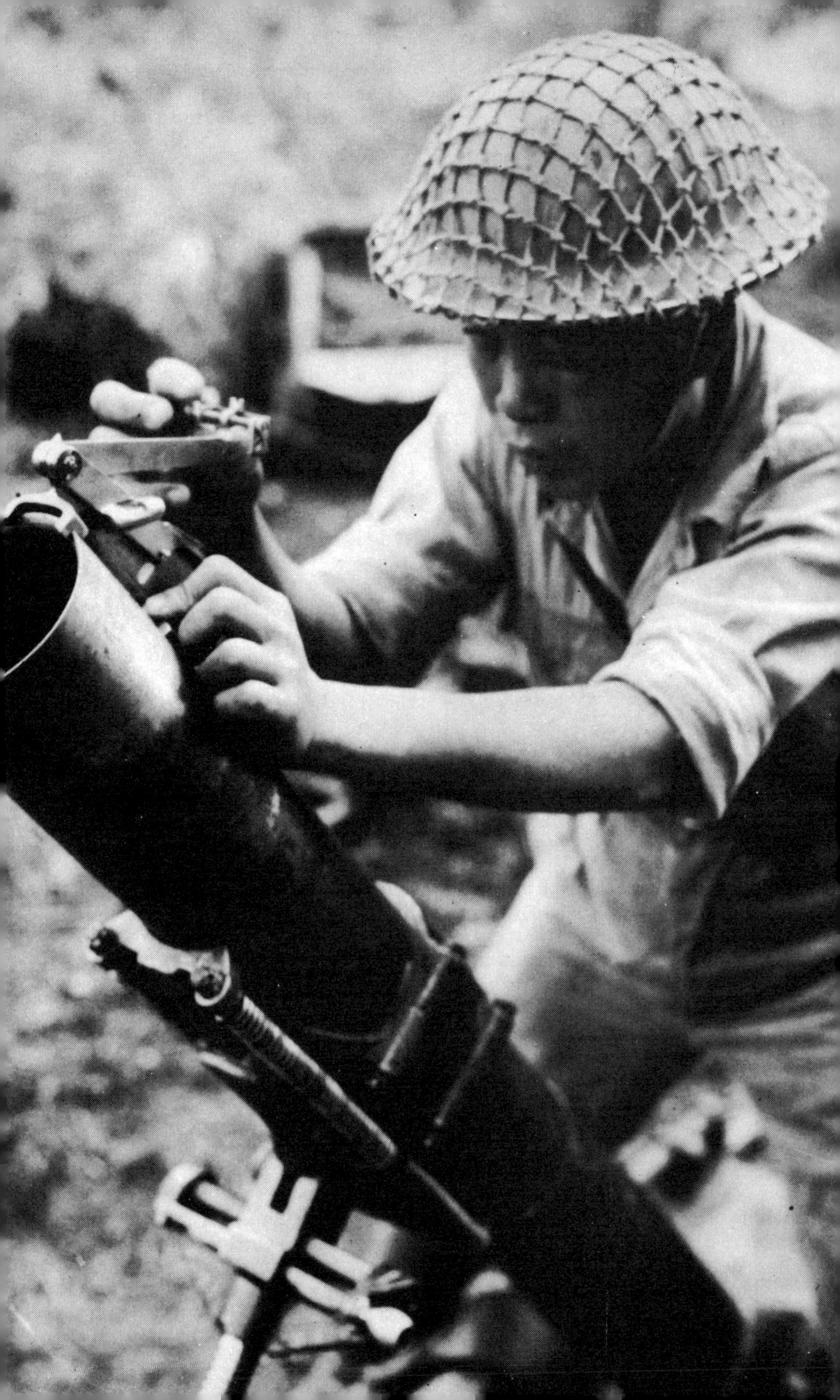

on 4th December, Rees's swift moving 19th Division, without waiting for its artillery, moved through the Zibyu-Taungdan Range and made contact with 36th Division at Indaw on 16th December. Intelligence reports and captured documents indicated that Slim had misread the Japanese intentions and that they were retreating across the Irrawaddy. In the new circumstances Slim made the courageous decision of changing his initial plan completely. He knew he could now rely on his divisions to turn smartly to his orders. He decided to switch his main force to attempt to capture the great administration base of Meiktila, across the Irrawaddy and seventy miles south of Mandalay. The Meiktila-Thazi airfield, supply, ordnance, hospital and communications complex was the key administrative centre for both the Japanese Thirty-third and Fifteenth Armies. After Rangoon, it was the most important area in Burma. Its capture would undermine the Burma Area Army's whole defence and throw it into confusion. Slim had tanks superior to the enemy's and he could apply them best in the dry, flat open sandy country around Meiktila in the dry zone. His air component (221st Group HQ was situated alongside his own and worked hand in glove) could also be applied most effectively in that open country during the perfect weather of the dry season.

Slim made this change of plan on his own and it was a masterpiece. The main factor was that Slim knew that he could now rely on his energetic, resourceful and 'offensive-minded' commanders and their troops to carry out his ambitious plan. His knowledge of the country now stood him in good stead. He would not use parachute troops, although they were available, as he thought they would tie his hands.

He would press on from the north to

Chinese soldier checks the sights of a 4.2mm mortar before firing

Lieutenant-General Oliver Leese, brought from Italy to command ALFSEA (Allied Land Forces South East Asia) in November 1944

keep the Japanese occupied and facing north, while half his army would move down the Gangaw valley to Pauk and Pakokku, cross the Irrawaddy, and advance rapidly across the wide open dry country to Meiktila which it would seize with a *coup de main*. His plan was nearly ruined by the withdrawal of seventy-five American Transport aircraft to increase the airlift to the constantly complaining Chiang Kai-shek (and his wife, who had great influence in the United States and who hated the British).

On 16th December Slim warned Oliver Leese of his impending change of plan and on the 18th gave him an outline of his new plan which he called 'Extended Capital'. He also issued his instructions to Messervy and Stopford. It meant a change of corps for some divisions.

His outline plan was all-embracing and ambitious. Accompanied by Stilwell's Northern Combat Command, he would destroy the enemy forces in

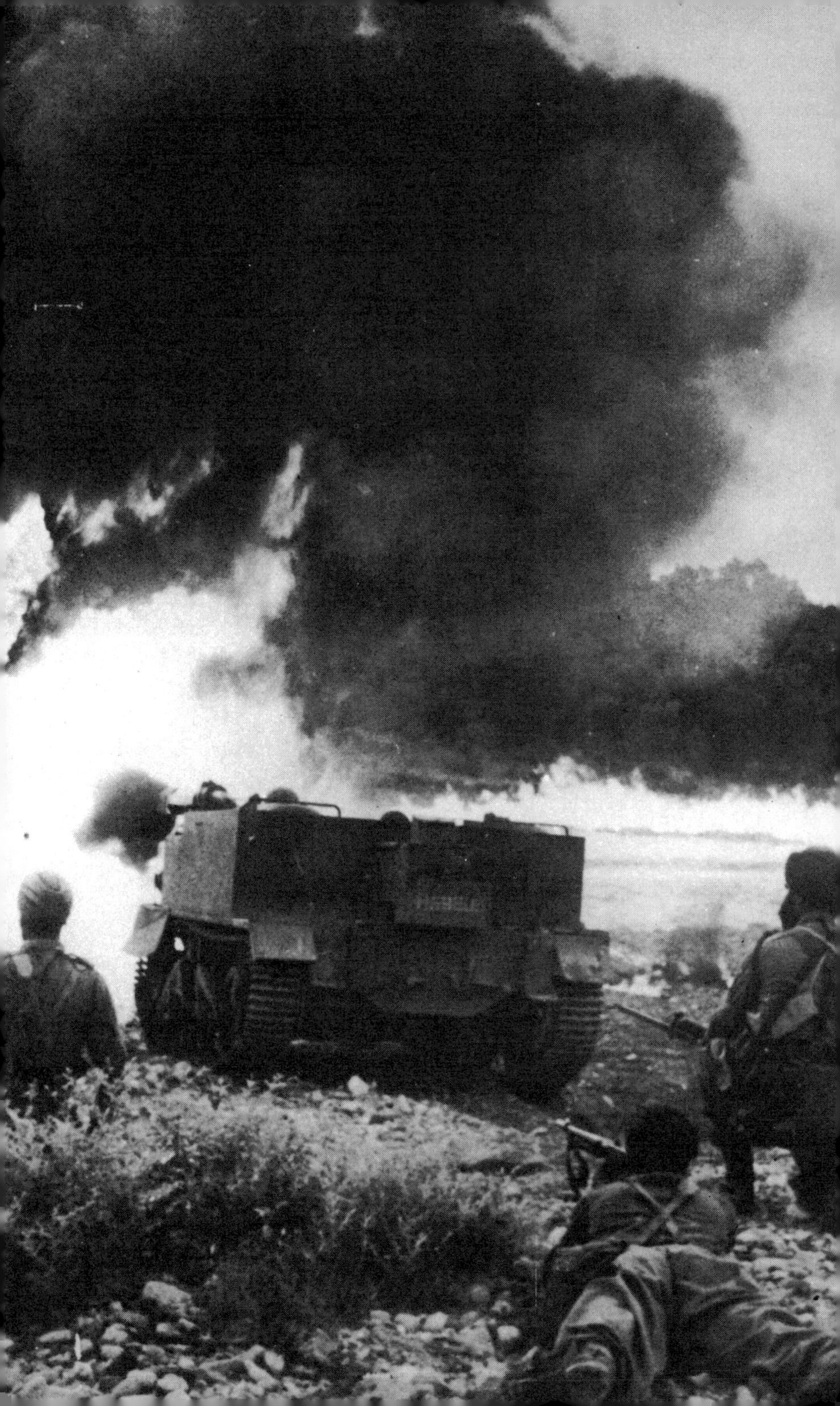

Burma. He would advance to the line Henzada-Nyaunglebin (300 miles south of Mandalay and seventy miles north of Rangoon) and he would then seize a port in South Burma. He would need 17th Division, now refitting in India. He would retain East African 28th Brigade and 255th Tank Brigade with its Sherman tanks.

He had four months before the monsoon to carry out his plan and if he had not gained a southern port by then his whole force would be in jeopardy and entirely reliant on air supply from Assam at increasingly long distances.

To fool the Japanese Slim organised a strategic deception plan. A dummy IV Corps with live wireless sets sending out spurious signals was set up at Tamu. All units of IV Corps were to maintain wireless silence. The East African Brigade would lead IV Corps's advance simulating East African 11th Division. Alternative crossing places of the Irrawaddy would be reconnoitred as a last minute tactical deception to confuse the enemy.

The boundary between the two corps, with IV Corps to the west, would be the Chindwin River which Stopford could use as a waterway. Between XXXIII Corps in the centre and the Stilwell Northern Combat Command, would be the Irrawaddy.

The Japanese were to be destroyed between the hammer of Stopfords XXXIII Corps coming down on Mandalay and the armoured anvil of Messervy's IV Corps at Meiktila. Stopford would have 2nd, 19th and 20th Divisions with 254th Tank Brigade (Lee-Grants and Stuarts) and Messervy 7th, 17th Divisions and East African 28th Brigade with 255th Tank Brigade (Shermans).

Stopford began his advance from Kalewa on 24th December; 20th Division moved on Monywa and 2nd Division on Shwebo. 19th Division was also heading for Shwebo. By 14th January 20th Division had reached Monywa. However, bad weather on the Chindwin had held up supplies and the all-important tanks (now that they were coming into the dry zone), and caused Stopford to call a halt for a whole fortnight.

But his aggressive 19th Division under Rees had crossed the Irrawaddy at Thabeikkyin and had advanced east of the Irrawaddy south to Kyaukmyaung, thus penetrating the Japanese Irrawaddy line. The Japanese reacted violently with fanatical attacks from their depleted 15th and 53rd Divisions. So Stopford's halt was not a complete waste of time.

British 36th Division was directed by Stilwell on the ruby mines of Mogok across the Irrawaddy, so 19th Division only was available to attack Mandalay.

Stopford decided to attack Mandalay from the north-west and from the south. 19th Division would come direct down the east bank of the Irrawaddy. 2nd Division with the tanks would come down the railway from Shwebo to Sagaing, nearly opposite Mandalay, and cross in that vicinity. 20th Division would cross near Myinmu and drive on Kyaukse a few miles south of Mandalay.

Messervy's IV Corps had 150 miles to go over bullock cart tracks down the disease-ridden Gangaw valley. The East African Brigade, with their mules, set a fast pace initially. Then 7th Division passed through them and a brigade reached Pauk on 26th January, four days ahead of schedule, having met no resistance. The Japanese did not appreciate the significance of the few reports that they received of this advance.

One of Messervy's main difficulties was to bring forward the boating equipment for the operation and to train his inexperienced battalions in an assault crossing. Messervy's plan was to use 7th Division to make a bridgehead over the mile wide river, and to use 17th Division and the tank brigade to make the dash to Meiktila.

Flame-throwing bren carriers ('Wasps') in training with Sikh infantry

ALLIED LINE on about 1st DECEMBER 1944

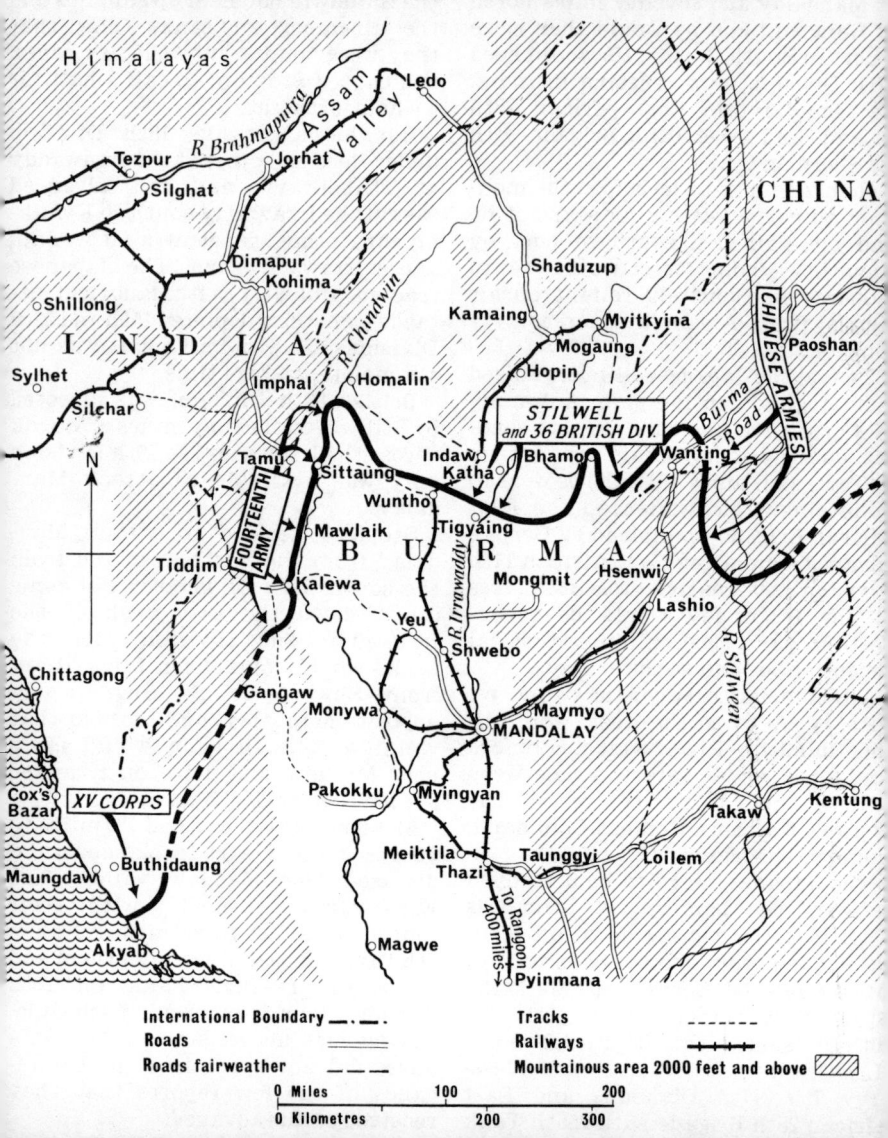

CAPITAL and EXTENDED CAPITAL

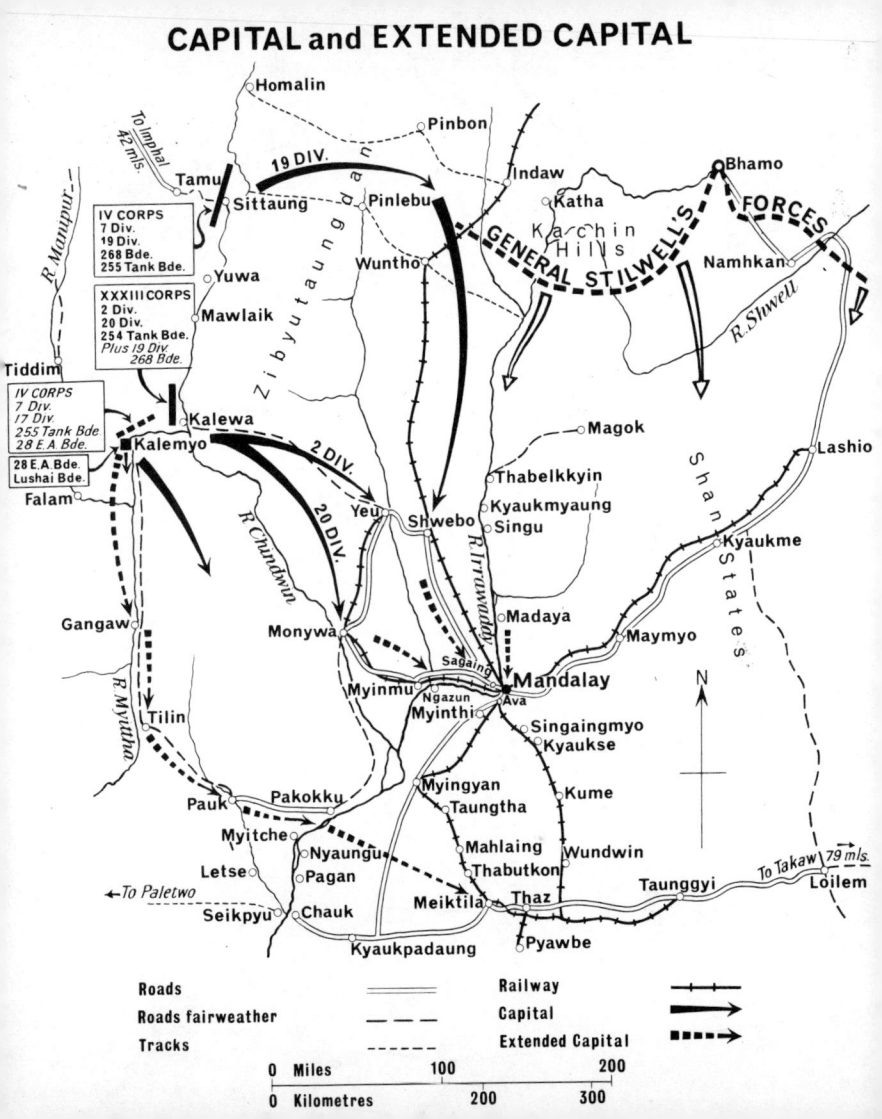

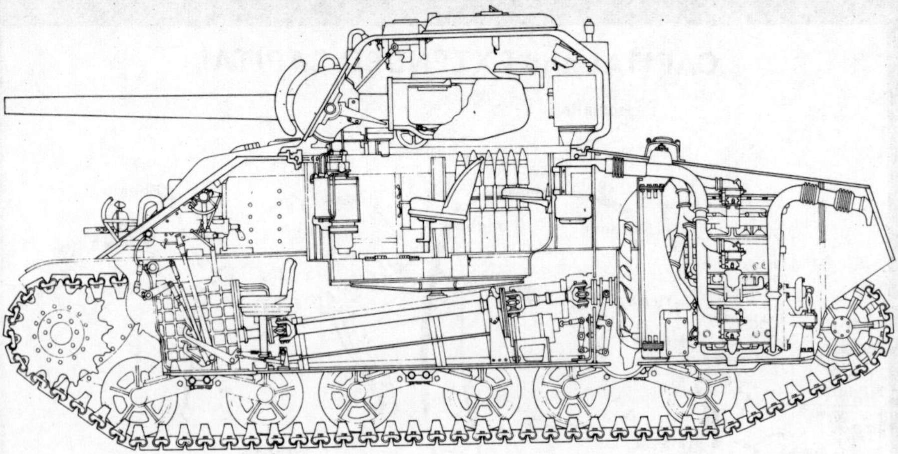

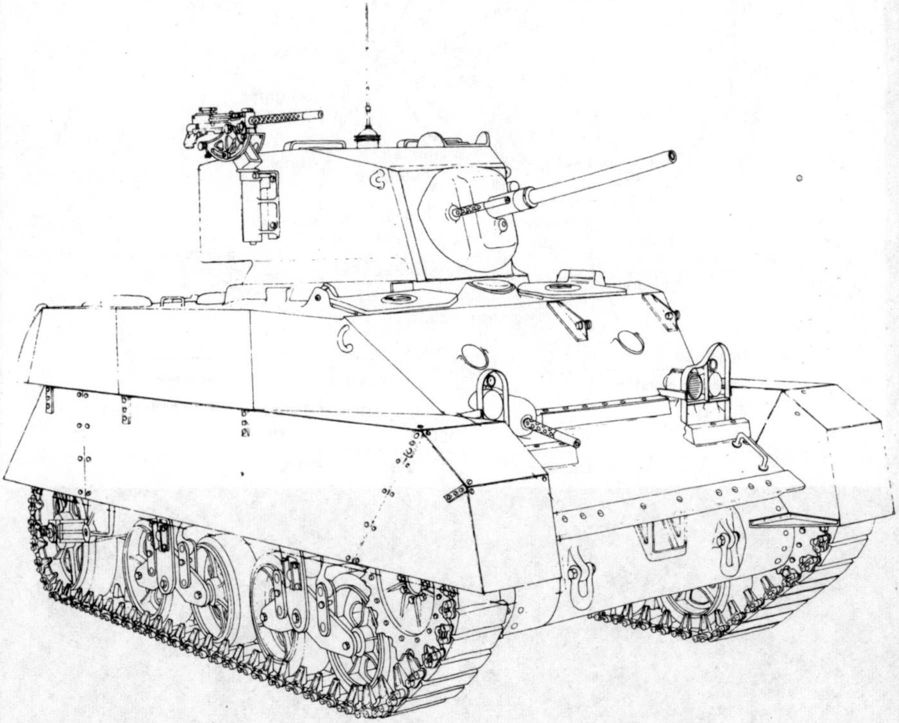

The US M4A4 General Sherman medium tank. This tank, the most famous and successful American armoured fighting vehicle of the Second World War, was developed to utilise as many components of the earlier M3 General Grant as possible and then replace it on the production lines. About 49,000 were built between 1942 and 1945. The type was an immediate success, though the fact that its armament proved adequate in the Sherman's earlier career led to a certain American reluctance to hamper production by improving it later in the war, though this was definitely needed. A total of 7,499 Sherman M4A4's was built, though the type was the first to be phased out of production, as the US Ordnance Department considered its engine to be too complicated. The M4A4 was known as the Sherman V by the British. *Weight:* 32.6 tons. *Crew:* 5. *Armament:* One 75mm M3 gun, plus one .5-inch and two .3-inch Browning machine guns. *Armour:* 85mm maximum, 20mm minimum. *Engine:* One Chrysler 30-cylinder 5-bank inline, 425hp. *Speed:* 23mph maximum. *Range:* 100 miles. *Ford:* 3 feet. *Trench:* 7 feet 6 inches. *Step:* 2 feet. *Length:* 21 feet 6 inches. *Width:* 8 feet 9 inches. *Height:* 9 feet 5 inches

The US M3 General Stuart (Honey) light tank. This was the first US tank to see service in the second World War, and soon earned itself considerable admiration as a roomy and reliable fighting vehicle. It was designed to have complete components changed in the event of mechanical failure, rather than having them repaired *in situ* this making servicing a speedy business. The type's chief failing was its lack of range. *Weight:* 12.3 tons. *Crew:* 4. *Armament:* One 3mm gun with 103 rounds and three .3-inch Browning machine guns with 8,270 rounds. *Armour:* 1.5-inch hull front and turret front; 1.25-inch turret sides; 1-inch hull sides and rear; .5-inch turret top; .35-inch hull top and bottom. *Engine:* One Continental 7-cylinder radial, 250hp. *Speed:* 36mph. *Range:* 70 miles. *Ford:* 3 feet. *Trench:* 6 feet. *Step:* 2 feet. *Length:* 16 feet 9 inches. *Width:* 7 feet 4 inches. *Height:* 7 feet 7 inches

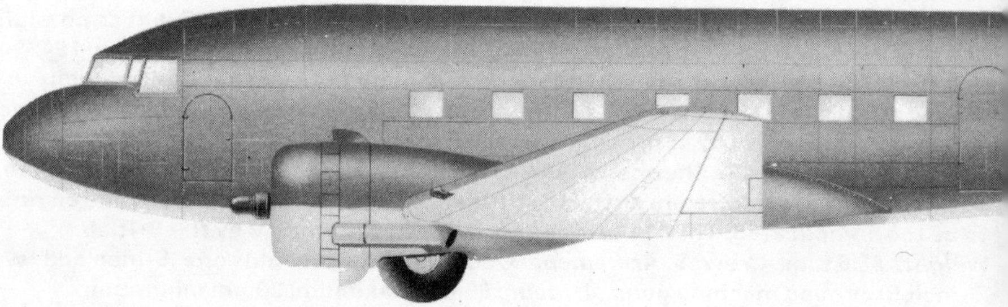

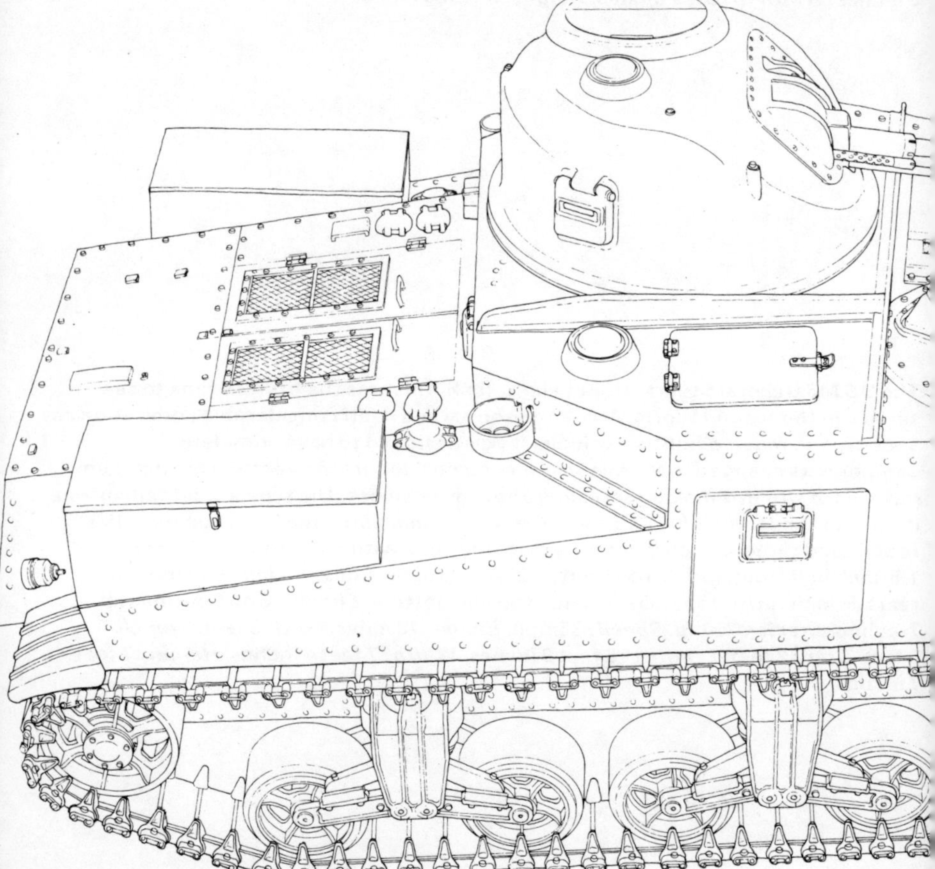

The Douglas C-53 Skytrooper. This military version of the famous DC-3 prewar airliner, together with the other main version, the C-47 Skytrain, was one of the great war-winning aircraft, and served with particular distinction in South-East Asia, flying supplies 'over the hump' to China and supplying forces operating behind the Japanese lines, as well as carrying out a multitude of less glamorous but equally important transport tasks. The chief difference between the C-47 and C-53 was that the former was designed as a cargo aircraft, and was therefore fitted with a reinforced floor and double doors on the port side of the fuselage. The C-53 was intended as a personnel transport, and was more similar to the prewar DC-3. The type was known generically as the Dakota by the RAF. *Engines:* Two Pratt & Whitney R-1830 Twin Wasp radials, 1,200hp each. *Speed:* 230mph at 8,800 feet. *Ceiling:* 24,100 feet. *Range:* 1,350 miles. *Load:* 28 troops (C-53) or 7,500lbs of cargo (C-47). *Weight empty/loaded:* 16,976/29,000lbs. *Span:* 95 feet. *Length:* 64 feet 5.5 inches. *Crew:* 4.

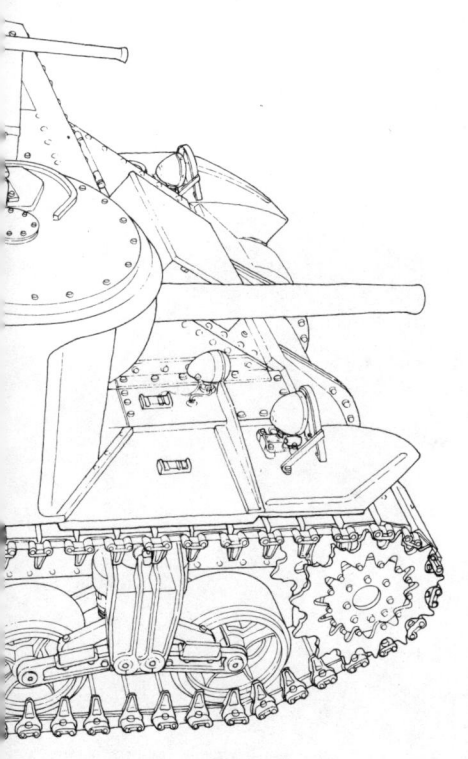

The US M3 General Grant medium tank. This was the Sherman's predecessor in the US tank forces, and was supplied in some numbers to the British, who used it first in North Africa and then in South-East Asia. It was adequately armed and armoured, reliable and well equipped, but was very high (and had to expose a lot of itself before the main armament could fire over the crests of hills) and carried much of its ammunition high in the turret, where it was very vulnerable to anti-tank fire. All in all, however, it was a great improvement on the current British generation of tanks. *Weight:* 27 tons. *Crew:* 6/7. *Armament:* One 75mm gun with 46 rounds, one 37mm gun with 178 rounds and three .3-inch Browning machine guns with 9,200 rounds. *Armour:* 2.25-inch turrent front, sides and rear; 2-inch hull front; 1.5-inch hull sides and rear; 1-inch hull bottom; .8-inch turret top; and .5-inch hull top. *Engine:* One Continental 9-cylinder radial, 340hp. *Speed:* 26 mph. *Range:* 120 miles. *Ford:* 3 feet 4 inches. *Trench:* 6.2 feet. *Step:* 2 feet. *Length:* 18 feet 6 inches. *Width:* 8 feet 11 inches. *Height:* 10 feet 3 inches

Above: 19th Division swim mules across the 800 yard-wide Irrawaddy
Below: Signaller Lance-Corporal Braithwaite with 7th Division at Pauk

Above: General Slim meets victorious British and Indian troops during his flying visit to Meiktila. *Below:* 2nd British Division ferry tanks across the mile-wide Irrawaddy at Ngazun below Mandalay

British Commandos mop up at Akyab

Landing party at Ramree Island

Nyaungu, south of Pakokku, was chosen as the site for the crossing. This happened to be on the boundary between the Japanese Fifteenth and Twenty-eighth Armies and so, by chance, could not have been better chosen. Nyaungu was defended by the rather ineffective remains of the Indian National Army.

Slim now held the initiative. The very width of the Irrawaddy concealed his intentions. He had advanced on a wide front to the Irrawaddy and could choose his crossing site while the Japanese had to cover a great length of river. Slim's only anxiety was the availability of boats and the water training of his men, especially the field engineers who would be primarily responsible.

By 1st February XXXIII Corps had moved up on to the Irrawaddy so Slim was poised for action. 19th Division to the north of Mandalay was still the main attraction to the Japanese.

On 12th February Stopford's 20th Division started to cross at Myinmu thirty miles west along the river from Mandalay. This attracted the Japanese. In succession on the next night Messervy's 7th Division, ninety miles further south, launched its assault crossing. 20th Division obtained a bridgehead which formed a honey-pot attracting violent reactions from the Japanese 33rd Division for the next three weeks until the 5th March. This diversion, as it turned out to be, allowed IV Corps to cross almost uneventfully. Rees's ebullient 19th Division advanced to within twenty miles of Mandalay.

Stopford's 2nd Division had had to wait for 20th Division boats and rafts but succeeded, after some hitches, in making a crossing on 21st February at Ngazun within fifteen miles of Mandalay.

So by the beginning of March 1945 Slim had crossed the Irrawaddy in four places, threatened the communication centre and ancient capital of Mandalay, and still the Japanese had not fully realised the potential of his southern envelopment onto Meiktila which was the key to the whole plan.

Slim deserves every credit for this ambitious plan, and the determination and drive with which he made his corps and divisions carry it through, due primarily to his own choice of aggressive commanders. Stopford was still full of Staff College training, always deliberate, wanting to tidy everything up before he made a move and never risking a quick coup. But he was sure and it was perhaps necessary to have some one of his bulldog tenacity to offset the cavalry dash of Messervy.

Before the battles which resulted in the capture of Mandalay and Meiktila, the high command were already planning for the next steps. One major divergence between the attitude of the Chiefs of Staff (even Mountbatten) and Slim was that the former seemed obsessed with the capture of named towns while Slim was still, quite rightly, intent on destroying the Japanese armies. This made his views on administrative problems different and more practical than those of his superiors. He knew that he could take administrative risks with a victorious army and that the morale of the enemy counted for more than numbers on a map. Slim was the practical commander in the field and he knew men. They were not just 'software', as they appeared in Washington.

Mountbatten had been told on 5th February that his first job was 'to liberate Burma at the earliest date' and that he should 'aim at the accomplishment of your object with the forces at present at your disposal.'

By now Akyab and Taungup on the Burma coast had fallen unopposed to Christison, lessening the air supply and support flights and making possible a route to supply Slim from Taunup to Prome. Mountbatten passed orders on to Oliver Leese that he could now have all the resources available for the 'Dracula' plan for a landing at Rangoon. So Slim's advance was being assisted by these landings and

Sherman tank of Probyn's Horse during the dash to capture Meiktila

Meiktila

Major-General Cowan, victor of Meiktila, in conference with his brigadiers

5.5-inch gun in action against the walls of Fort Dufferin, Mandalay

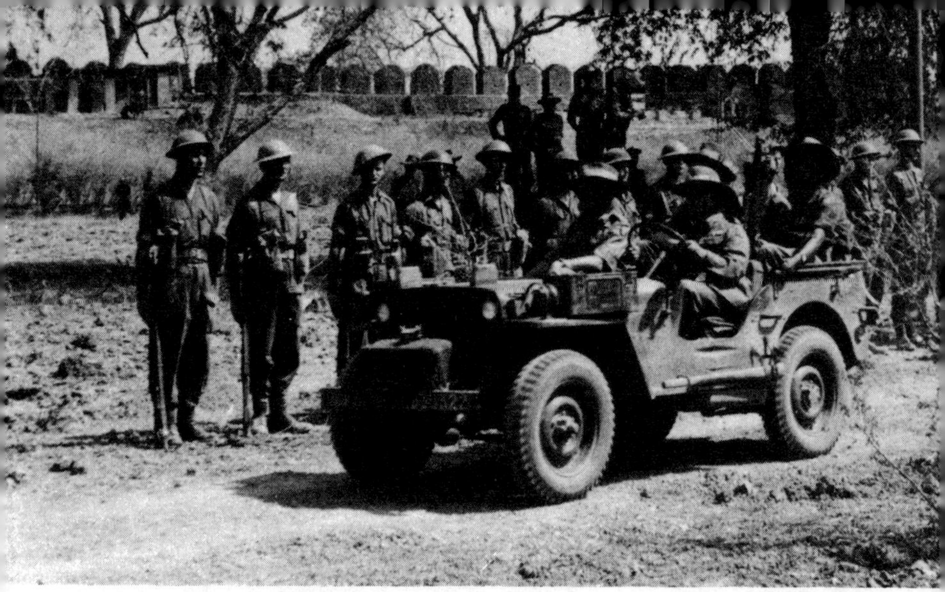

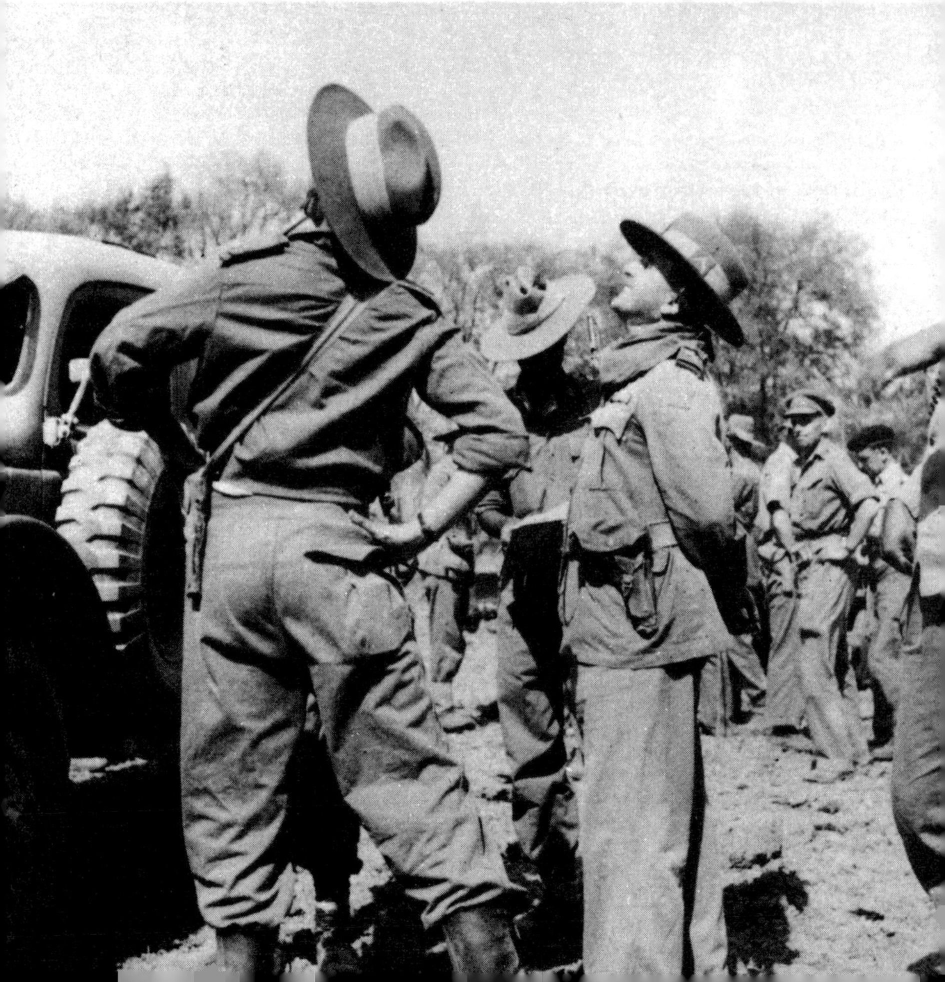

General Slim returns to Mandalay two years later

further planned landings to his west and south.

The Japanese were confused as to British intentions. Their Intelligence system seems to have collapsed as they retreated, as so often happens, and they were now blind. They thought that 19th Division was going east and not to Mandalay. The various landings had thrown them into confusion. On 13th February the Japanese 2nd Division was ordered to go to Indo-China to repel expected American landings there, accompanied by the 5th Air Division the remains of which comprised the whole Japanese air effort in Burma. They felt that IV Corps's southern approach was a Chindit-type raid and not a main thrust. Out of all this they decided to concentrate on a counterattack on 20th Division bridgehead at Myinma. Tokyo had, in fact, left the Japanese in Burma to their fate with the sole role of tying up as many Allied troops, aircraft and landing craft as possible to prevent their being switched to the main front in the Pacific.

Slim was also considering what to do after the capture of Meiktila. He

Major-General Rees, 19th Division, watches as the Union Jack is hoisted over Fort Dufferin

felt that an advance down the plain to Rangoon would leave his long eastern flank open to counterattack, so he contemplated sending part of XXXIII Corps into the Shan States. Everything he told Leese, depended on his getting enough air supply, and he presented his air requirements. Leese approved them.

On 18th February, after an initial setback to the East Africans further south, Messervy ordered the whole of his 17th Division and his tank brigade to cross the Irrawaddy into the bridgehead he had already gained at Nyaungu. Meiktila, his goal, was eighty miles away across sandy scrub country cut up by dry riverbeds. On 21st February 17th Division started its move. Evans's 7th Division was ordered at the same time to advance towards the oil town of Chauk in the south, and capture Myingyan to the north east. Cowan's 17th Division, with its tanks, overcoming some quite stiff opposition en route, reached the outskirts of Meiktila. On 1st March Cowan attacked. By evening Meiktila had fallen along with a most useful airfield on the eastern edge of the town. Patrols probing to Thazi and Pyawbwe to the south encountered enemy. So was completed the most audacious and important part of Slim's plan.

Slim himself had taken some hard knocks while awaiting the fall of Meiktila, but he had refused to allow these shocks to deflect him from his plan.

On 23rd February Slim was told of an imperious demand by Generalissimo Chiang Kai-shek for the return of all United States and Chinese forces under Stilwell's Northern Area Combat Command (NACC) to take part in an offensive in China. This would relieve the Japanese 18th and 56th division opposing NACC of all opposition except 36th Division and they

ADVANCE to RANGOON

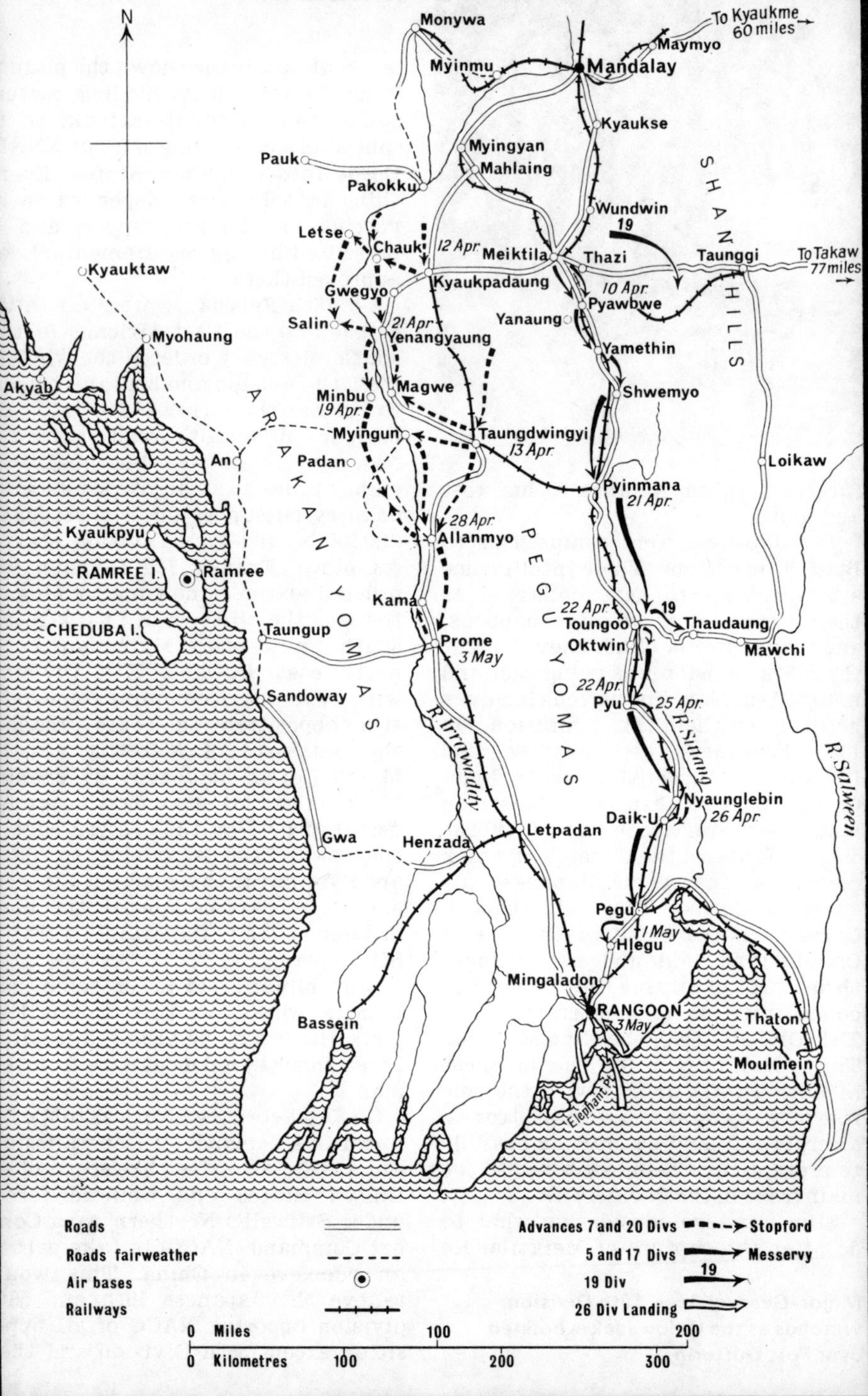

could turn on Fourteenth Army. Mountbatten had to take stern measures and arrange the cancellation of the move of these troops and most of the transport aircraft. But, while he was intent on the completion of an audacious plan in which supply was the key, this brouhaha had made Slim's administrative heart flutter. But he was an old campaigner now and he had shown no outward signs of unease.

Slim, true to form and carrying out what he considered was a commander's essential duty, flew forward first to visit Stopford at Monywa; and then with Messervy to Thabutkon near Meiktila to visit Cowan, where they watched a battle in progress. This battle of manoeuvre with tanks at one time enveloped the army commander's party, two of whom were wounded, but the army commander, corps commander and divisional commander remained imperturbable, upright and unscathed. This incident had a great boosting effect on the front line troops' morale.

Cowan was now faced with the inevitable Japanese counterattack. From what he had seen on the spot, Slim decided to move up his reserve division, the 5th, for Messervy's benefit, leaving one air transportable brigade at Imphal ready to be flown in to Meiktila. Cowan, in the meantime, decided on an aggressive defence of Meiktilla, attacking all Japanese approaching Meiktila as vigorously as possible, and leaving only a small garrison in the town.

The deliberate Stopford, having seen that his bridgeheads were secure, made plans for the step by step capture of Mandalay. 19th Division would attack from the north. 2nd Division would advance along the Irrawaddy to attack from the south and south-west. 20th Division would sweep further east to attack from the south and south-east.

19th Division soon penetrated the town but were held up by the battlements of Fort Dufferin which required heavy artillery and air bombardment to reduce. 20th Division made good progress, but 2nd Division's direct advance was held up among the pagodas of the ancient capital of Ava, and by some minefields.

Mandalay was not being held strongly so Slim, realising that Meiktila was the nodal point of the battle, ordered 20th Division to send a column south towards Meiktila while 2nd Division remorselessly surrounded Mandalay from the south.

The Japanese had not recovered from their confusion and misdirected their counterattacks. There was little coordination between their forces south of Meiktila and those to the north. Eventually, however, they realised that Meiktila was the key, and they attacked 17th Division and the tank brigade from all directions. These attacks were not deliberate or coordinated and the British tanks wrought havoc on their infantry in the open. Cowan was reinforced by 5th Division's air transported brigade and was able to hold the vital airfield area.

Meanwhile 19th Division, aided by massive air strikes, captured Fort Dufferin and Mandalay on the 20th March. The communication centre of Myingyan was captured by Evans's 7th Division. The newly arrived 5th Division captured Taungtha between Meiktila and the Irrawaddy which had been occupied by the Japanese in order to cut off land routes to 17th Division. 5th Division then advanced to Meiktila. The outflanking movement was complete.

The extent of these battles for the Irrawaddy, Mandalay and Meiktila can be judged by the casualties. Fourteenth Army lost 10,500 wounded and killed with, in addition, 7,000 sick evacuated. The Japanese faced by tanks on open ground, overwhelming air support, and rejuvenated divisions, suffered far higher casualties and lost much of their artillery.

Slim deserves all praise for the success of his ambitious plan. During the retreat and subsequently he had always wanted to attack, but he had bottled up his desires until he had the commanders and troops whom he could trust to operate aggressively without looking over their shoulders. Air supply, developed by Wingate and Stilwell, had made this possible, and the air force should rightly take much of the praise for this great success. But it was Slim who took the risk and it was Slim who succeeded. Messervy, Cowan and Rees were most willing instruments of aggression and their infantry and tanks, by their tactical skill on the battlefield, completed the vital workaday part of the job – and suffered the casualties, heat, dust and disease.

Slim had been anticipating his next move long before the capture of Meiktila and the fall of Mandalay. The monsoon loomed ahead and it was essential to capture Rangoon beforehand, or his troops might be left without supplies. But Slim still realised that the defeat of the Japanese was his main object and not the capture of country. His forward plans gave the Japanese no respite or time to recover.

Christison's XV Corps was developing its unopposed capture of Akyab and Ramree Island but had failed to cut off 54th Division's escape to the Irrawaddy. Slim urged Leese to get him to capture Rangoon as Fourteenth Army moved south.

Slim had given orders to Stopford's XXXIII Corps, first to extend his left flank to clear the Maymyo area which had been the location of the Headquarters Burma Area Army, and then to move south on a wide front from Nyaungu on the Irrawaddy to Meiktila and relieve Messervy's IV Corps. XXXIII Corps was then to advance down the Irrawaddy route via Prome to Rangoon, but with the task of cleaning up behind IV Corps on the way.

Messervy was stripping for action for his dash down the railway via Toungoo to Rangoon. He proposed, and Slim approved, that he should reorganise his force into a mobile mechanised/air transportable column of two divisions and a tank brigade.

At this time Slim's force had to be reduced in order to cut down air supply demands. Leese was looking forward to the planned landing operation called 'Zipper', on the Malaya coast which was intended to capture Singapore. Northern Area Combat Command was disbanded on 1st April and 36th Division began to concentrate, after its months with the American – Chinese forces in Mandalay.

It had become increasingly difficult to keep up the strength of these British divisions. Their morale was not helped by a crassly stupid ministerial statement in the House of Commons that all troops with three and a half years service abroad had now returned to Britain. Most of 2nd and 36th British Divisions had been abroad for over four years, and the statement merely referred to those who had been serving in the comparative 'luxury' of the Middle East and Italy, and not to the 'Forgotten Army'. A repatriation scheme named 'Python' was set up, politically designed to win votes in the pending general election, whereby troops who had served longer than a certain period overseas had to be sent home. The British units in Burma were virtually destroyed in the process, and the remanants of 2nd and 36th Divisions were flown out to India to assist in training reinforcements for a seaborne assault landing.

Messervy, therefore, received all the transport of these two divisions and organised his corps on a lorried basis. He had 320 miles to go and forty-five days before the monsoon to take Rangoon. Christison's sea and airborne attack on Rangoon was timed for the beginning of May.

To help administer the recaptured area of Burma, and to leave Slim to get on with his battle, that administrative 'king' General Snelling was brought in to look after Fourteenth Army's maintenance from India. Snelling had been Slim's competent right-hand man throughout the campaign, and, to change the analogy, acted like a second outside the ring while Slim boxed within.

Messervy's start was delayed for nine days by stubborn Japanese resistance at Pyawbwe. Then he was off. His plan was to capture airfields for resupply en route but to avoid any strong defences. He would leapfrog one division past another from airfield to airfield so that there was always one ready coiled in support and to receive airlanded supplies. Pyinmana was captured on 19th April. Toungoo airfields were taken on 22nd April and Pegu on 1st May. Messervy was now only fifty miles from Rangoon but some unseasonal heavy rain held up the advance of his tanks.

Stopford's advance down the Irrawaddy was more sober and deliberate, as was his wont. His task was to clear up and not leave undefeated pockets of enemy who might concentrate and become a nuisance later. Stopford had to protect the more spectacular Messervy's right flank. He captured Chauk on 18th April; the oilfields of Magwe and Yenanyaung on 21st April; Allanmyo on the Irrawaddy on 28th April and entered Prome on 3rd May – which was a rapid advance for a 'cautious' commander. The Japanese sought safety in the forested but waterless Pegu Yomas where they became the ragged survivors of a once proud army.

On 1st May Gurkha parachutists dropped on Elephant Point outside Rangoon and overcame all opposition. Christison's seaborne landings were again not opposed and soon it became obvious that Rangoon was not defended. General Kimura had ordered its evacuation on 29th/30th April and directed the garrison to escape via Pegu, now held by Messervy. Messervy held a key position here and its retention was the final straw in the dissolution of the Japanese Army in Burma.

THE MALARIOUS AREAS OF BURMA

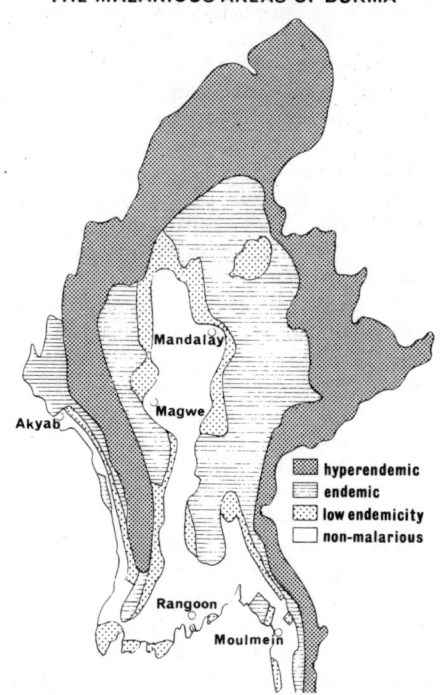

hyperendemic
endemic
low endemicity
non-malarious

IV Corps and Christison's Fifteenth Army met at Hlegu, halfway between Rangoon and Pegu on 6th May and Slim had completed his plan of conquest of Burma.

Both Corps had further work to do to mop up the remnants (about 6,000), of four divisions in the Yomas, and a similar number east of the Sittang River. These operations were intensive and to the junior officers carrying them out, because it became a junior officer war, very exciting; for many reinforcements it was their first action. But for the High Command it was just 'mopping up'.

By the time fighting stopped with the Japanese surrender in August 1945, the war in Burma had lasted forty-four months, and Slim had been actively engaged for all but a few of these. It included fighting over some of the most difficult country of the war, against the most fanatical enemy. But though sickness casualties were very high in Burma compared with other theatres, battle casualties were fairly low, considering the number of troops engaged, as the chart below shows.

Slim assumed command of all forces in Burma including Christison's XV Corps on the 6th May 1945. This was the start of a series of moves and manoeuvres amongst the high command. The protagonists were Leese and Slim, with Christison being Leese's protégé.

Stopford was given command of all forces in Burma as Commander of a new Twelfth Army, while Slim moved his rear HQ Fourteenth Army all the way back to Delhi, whence his Indian Army support had come. This occurred on 14th May.

A scene similar to Irwin's attempt to oust Slim had taken place. Oliver Leese had called Slim to his headquarters, congratulated him on his wonderful success and suggested that he now needed a rest as he had been fighting almost without cease for over three years since early 1942. Now that Burma was conquered the war would become one of combined operations and naturally Slim had not had the time or experience for this art. He suggested, therefore, that Slim should take a rest and await further posting.

Mountbatten and Leese were now planning the invasion of Malaya, an operation called 'Zipper' which was to be undertaken by Lieutenant-General Ouvry Roberts, an energetic, intelligent Royal Engineer, in command of a newly formed XXXIV Corps. He had previously commanded 81st (West African) Division in the Arakan.

SEAC Joint Planning Staff had chosen the Port Dickson-Port Swettenham area in Malaya as their objective. They considered that the beaches nearby at Morib and Sepang were the only ones suitable for a quick discharge of vehicles. However, rapid changes of command at the top were to cause the participating generals so much concern about their own positions that they did not appear to take sufficient interest to check the facts on which Operation Zipper was plan-

	Killed	Wounded	Missing	Total
Officers	947	1,837	307[2]	3,091
British Other Ranks	5,037	10,687	2,507[2]	18,231
Indian Other Ranks	8,235	28,873[1]	8,786[2]	45,894
African Other Ranks	858	3,208[1]	200	4,266
Burmese Other Ranks	249	126	3,052[3]	3,427
Total	15,326	44,731	14,852	74,909
2nd Chindit	(1,034)	(2,302)	(450)	(3,786)

(1) The high proportion of Indian and African wounded or killed is because these troops obtained pensions for wounds and therefore kept meticulous records, whereas the British did not report minor wounds. (2) Many of the missing were from the Retreat in 1942. (3) Many Burmese soldiers on the Retreat simply returned to their homes in Burma; after the Retreat, their numbers are included in 'Indian Other Ranks'. (4) The Second Chindit operation casualties are included in the totals. (5) American and Chinese army casualties could not be confirmed.

ned. Zipper was to become 'unzipped' on the day of landing.

Slim, discontented with his treatment after the part he had played in the conquest of Burma, decided to go on leave to England in early June and present his case there. On 1st July he was promoted General.

Slim appealed in person to the Army Council as was now his right, and it was decided that Leese should be the one to leave, with Slim taking his place.

On 6th July Oliver Leese vacated his appointment as Commander-in-Chief ALFSEA and Christison became officiating Commander-in-Chief in his place. Japan surrendered on the 14th August. Mountbatten returned to Ceylon after a short visit to London on the same date. Slim arrived back on 15th August and took over command of ALFSEA from Christison the following day. Christison did not get an army command but took two steps down and left to resume command of his old XV Corps.

Slim now rather drops out of the picture. Perhaps Leese's view was right and Slim *was* tired, or he was incapable of seeing the wider picture including the Combined Operations side of subsequent military affairs. The war moved from his safe base in India and he was rather lost in the jungle of postwar occupational politics in South East Asia.

On 17th August, Mountbatten outlined his plans for the occupation of the now widely extended South East Asia Command which included Burma, Malaya, the Netherland East Indies, Siam and Southern Indo-China. Slim passed on Mountbatten's instructions to his generals the same day, amplified by a further administrative instruction on the 23rd which had been prepared for him by the ALFSEA Chief of Staff whilst he was away in England.

Briefly, Fourteenth Army would clear up Burma and hand it over to IV Corps (Messervy) which would then become Burma Command. On 10th August Sir Miles Dempsey replaced Stopford in command of Fourteenth Army. Dempsey became overall commander for the occupation of Malaya and Singapore including operation 'Zipper' which was still planned to take place as an exercise. Fourteenth Army, based on Singapore, would then take command of the Netherland East Indies. Twelfth Army (where Stopford had moved to take over Command) would go to Bangkok and take command of Siam and Indo-China.

Most of the planning for operation Zipper had taken place before Slim assumed command of ALFSEA; but as overall commander Slim himself must take some responsibility for the near disaster of the operation. He had approved both the carrying out of the operation after it had become unnecessary, and the date.

Zipper took place on 9th September, twenty-six days after the Japanese surrender. One reason for it was to impress the Malays. Two battleships, four cruisers, six escort carriers and fifteen destroyers escorted the 'D day' convoys to their respective beaches and the first flight of landing craft moved onto their appointed beaches on time.

At Morib, not one of the first twenty vehicles reached the beach across the 100-yard muddy water gap without assistance from recovery vehicles. Fifty vehicles were 'drowned' on the first day. From Divisional Headquarters, only one jeep reached the shore. The area selected for de-waterproofing the vehicle (after landing) was in fact quite inaccessible to vehicles, being separated from the road by a deep boggy ditch and water pipeline raised a foot off the ground. When vehicles and tanks eventually got ashore, they quickly bogged down on the soggy roadside verges.

Conditions at Sepang beach turned out to be better and a more suitable beach was found in place of Morib. Port Dickson was occupied on the 10th. Mountbatten, Slim and Roberts

Above: Frontier Force Rifles hoist the Union Jack at Prome. *Below:* Landing craft on Rangoon River on the day of liberation

(XXXIV Corps) visited 25th Division Headquarters (Hawthorn) at Klang on 11th September before it moved to Kuala Lumpur for a ceremonial entry on 13th September.

However, the Official History suggests that even if there had been an opposed landing, the 26,000-strong Japanese forces spread out all over Malaya (a further 70,000 were in Singapore) without any air support could not have successfully resisted a determined invasion, although troops landed on the Morib beaches would have had to be withdrawn, and a quick and sound revision of the plans made.

'Python' had so decimated the British divisions that all these post-war moves in South East Asia were carried out by Indian divisions (with only a comparatively few British specialised units accompanying them). So the Indian Army could take no pride in operation 'Zipper' except in so far as they had made the best of a badly planned job. The schemings and musical chairs of the high command in South East Asia, from which Slim does not emerge unmuddied, must have been partly to blame for this bad planning.

Finally, IV Corps closed down on 1st October and began disbandment. Twelfth Army became Burma Command on 1st November. Fourteenth Army became Malaya Command on the same date. XV Corps became Netherland East India Command on 1st October. XXXIV Corps, which undertook Zipper, closed on 1st November and was disbanded.

British troops 'spontaneously' cheer the news of the Japanese surrender

Slim handed over ALFSEA to Dempsey on 8th November and departed to England to reconstitute and become Commandant of the Imperial Defence College. He was fifty-four.

He remained as Commandant until 1947. However, he did not get on with the Chief of the Imperial General Staff, Lord Montgomery, who thought of him as a 'Sepoy Soldier'. He retired in 1947 and took a job with British Railways. He was appointed a Deputy Chairman in 1948.

Slim came back to the army to replace Lord Montgomery as CIGS in 1948, a post which he held until 1952. He was appointed Field Marshal in 1949, which ensured him an income until his death on 14th December 1970 aged seventy-nine. He had been appointed Governor General of Australia from 1953 until 1958. He became Governor and Constable of the Tower of Windsor Castle in 1964 and remained there until shortly before his death. The funeral ceremony was held at Windsor Castle on 22nd December 1970 and was attended by thousands of his old comrades of all ranks.

Slim was not a great captain of war by any means. At a time when warfare was changing very rapidly, he was responsible for no great innovations in tactical method or strategic thought. Nor, unlike Wavell, was he quick to pick on any new means for outwitting the enemy. For exam-

Slim, Air Marshal Vincent, AOC 221 Group, and Major General Chambers,

Field-Marshal Sir William Slim at the Royal Hospital, Chelsea

General Sir William Joseph Slim with Field-Marshal Lord Montgomery

ple, he never liked to use special forces such as paratroops or commandos, and was probably the weaker for not realising their potential. He was reluctant to exploit the opportunities which Chindit-type operations made possible, and though he could have achieved nothing in that theatre of war without air supply, he was slow to put his whole trust in it. His deployment of troops was sound but rarely brilliant: only the capture of Meiktila in 1945 bears the mark of genius.

The qualities which he did possess were the unexciting ones of steadiness, perseverance and sound judgement. As an historian said of Blucher, Wellington's partner at Waterolo, Slim also was 'endowed with common sense, fiery energy and indomitable courage ... was defeated many times and had little knowledge of the higher arts and science of war ... Nevertheless on the battlefield his determination and personal courage and example was worth its weight in gold.' Perhaps Slim was not always as confident as he looked. Some rather panicky messages which he sent to his superiors during the Imphal battle detract from his reputation as a cool, calm general. But he still maintained the essential appearance of calm, and whatever uncertainty he may have felt did not leak down to his subordinates. This capacity to look the part was one of Slim's great assets, enabling him to make the best use of the abilities he possessed.

Slim's human qualities were just as important. In an area where the ratio of morale to the physical was more like 6 to 1 than the 3 to 1 ratio of Clausewitz's famous dictum, it was vital for troops to have confidence in their general. Slim did more than that. He inspired the loyalty and affection in soldiers of all races, a loyalty which welded the 'Forgotten Army' together, and handled his subordinate commanders well, even gaining the respect of a brilliant individualist like Wingate and of the difficult and anti-British Stilwell.

These attributes would not have been enough without the ability to learn, which transformed Slim from the mediocre brigadier of 1940 to the excellent army commander of 1945. The initial failure at Gallabat led him to be bolder, not more hesitant, in later attacks – even though he over-compensated at Deir-ez-Zor by using two brigades to take a weakly-held village. The retreat from Burma involved him in a new type of warfare, in which he was at first outclassed by the Japanese, but set himself to learn again – with results which appeared in his training schedules for VX Corps, the rescue operation in the Arakan in 1943, and his eventual appreciation of the role of air supply as a counter to Japanese penetration. This phase reached its crux in the Arakan and Imphal battles of 1944. Immediately afterwards, Slim showed astonishing resilience – after two years of defensive fighting – in going over to the offensive while the outcome at Imphal was still unclear. Only at the end does he appear to have been out of his depth, and to have lost confidence in himself, in the complex waters of South East Asian grand strategy.

A soldiers' general, Slim was a practical campaigner rather than a grand strategist. He was always prepared to improvise and get on with the job, rather than wait for perfection as some of his counterparts in Europe tended to do.

The Duke of Wellington once scathingly remarked of some of Napoleon's marshals that 'they planned their campaigns just as you might make a splendid set of harness. It looks very well, and answers very well, until it gets broken; and then you are done for. Now I make my campaign of ropes. If anything goes wrong, I tied a knot and went on'.

Slim, faced again and again with failure or lack of supplies, tied a knot and went on to victory. Probably no other British general of that era could, under such conditions, have achieved so much.

Bibliography

China-Burma-India Theater by Charles Romanus and Riley Sutherland (Dept. of the Army)
Defeat into Victory by Field-Marshal Viscount Slim (Cassell, London)
Golden Arrow by Brigadier M R Roberts (Gale & Polden, London)
Kōgun, the Japanese Army in the Pacific War by S Hyashi and A Coox (US Marine Corps)
Kohima by Arthur Swinson (Cassell, London)
The March on Delhi by A J Barker (Faber & Faber, London)
The War against Japan, vols 3 and 4, by S W Kirby (HMSO, London)